Ans

from the

Other Side

First published 2022

Copyright © Julie Ann Tyso 2022

Published under licence by Brown Dog Books and
The Self-Publishing Partnership Ltd, 10b Greenway Farm, Bath Rd, Wick, nr. Bath BS30 5RL

www.selfpublishingpartnership.co.uk

ISBN printed book: 978-1-83952-487-5
ISBN e-book: 978-1-83952-488-2

Cover design by Andrew Prescott
Internal design by Andrew Easton

Printed and bound in the UK

This book is printed on FSC certified paper

Answers
from the
Other Side

Julie Ann Tyso

BROWN
DOG
BOOKS

Dedication and Acknowledgements

This book is dedicated to everyone who wants answers to the big questions about what happens when we die. My hope is that these words bring an acceptance and peace that enable you to live your physical life to its full and natural conclusion in the clear knowledge that we are not just our bodies and our true essence survives our physical death.

This book would not exist without the considerable help, guidance and encouragement from souls residing on both sides of life. From the main direct spiritual contributor to my spiritual family and especially my late parents who support me always – there are no words to fully express my gratitude for all your love, encouragement and the faith you have shown in me.

I am so fortunate to be surrounded by wonderful family and friends in this life and without you, this book would not be in print. My dear husband, son, son-in-law, daughter and much-loved friends – old and new – you have all played an essential role, whether as a confidant and early reader, leveller, encourager or enabler; each and every contribution has been invaluable and I thank you all.

Contents

INTRODUCTION

I am not even sure what led me to sit in front of the computer on the morning of 25 October 2017 and begin to channel this book, but I felt a need to sit and share what I believe was being shared with me and take you all on this journey with me.

Yes, the desire to write a book one day had been in my mind on and off (more 'off') at different times in my life, but then, I assume many people feel like that. Many of us believe we have a book in us, but if I did then I certainly had no idea what mine might be!

I suddenly felt guided to do this now. The idea came to me over the course of a couple of days and it suddenly felt right to sit down and try. I decided that if I was going to give this a fair chance then I needed to allocate set times to work on it. I work better in the mornings, so getting up and sitting down in front of the computer at 8 am on the dot was what I decided to do. For the first time in my adult life I had spare time – not a massive amount, but some that I could allocate to this venture.

I have used handwritten journals to record my thoughts for as long as I can remember. Usually, entries are scribbled and consist of emotional outpourings which help me to understand what is going on around me. I sometimes write down a question in my journal and just wait to see what comes. I can honestly say that after an hour or so of journaling, my thoughts became clearer and I am able to look at my life in different ways. The process is valuable and I have often felt the answers I received were guided from a higher source. As life has become easier the journal entries become less frequent, but in times of confusion or sadness, they are my best friend.

My handwriting is difficult to read, even by me, so if I was going to do anything as involved as writing a book then capturing the words directly onto the computer was my only option. I could say that the idea came to me overnight, but honestly, the seed was somehow planted and I am not sure I was even party to the decision.

I seemed to be given very clear instructions about how to do this. I was to sit at the computer at 8 am two or three mornings a week, with the days being flexible on both sides, but they were always to be weekdays. It was made clear that the dictation would not be in chapter order and was to be edited later. I was to take dictation in a question/answer format and at the end of the session I was to print the file and save it in two places, with a new word document being started each day. The spiritual time allocated to me was a two-hour slot for each session, taking me up to 10 am. As the sessions progressed, I noted that dictation was winding down at around 9.15 am and in that time I had usually typed anything up to 2,500 words. That averaged out at over 33 words per minute: way beyond my normal typing speed and quite inexplicable!

At the end of each dictation, I would go back and check spelling errors, put my questions in italics,-indent them, print the hard copy and then save as directed. I put the paper copies in a clear-view plastic file and for the most part hardly looked at them again for weeks. I then went on with my day as normal. The dictation started on 25 October and ended on 31 January the following year, although there was further editing guidance after that date.

I decided not to tell anyone about this, other than my dear best friend and other half. Nothing I do seems to surprise him anymore and he takes everything in his stride. Occasionally, I would ask him to read something, but more often not. The odd thing is, as soon as I had finished the dictation, I could barely remember any of it! There were a couple of times when I attempted to explain to him what I had been told and I made a complete mess of it. When he did finally read a few sections, he helped me to confirm that this was not coming from me. In fact, he suggested that I might not even be posing the questions on my own. I had not even considered that. Coming from the person who knows me best, this was a revelation.

Although my name is on the front cover, I would have to argue that I am not the true author of this book. I provide translation and secretarial services, for want of a better expression. Although looking back on my life so far, I can see that a great deal of it has been in synchronistic preparation for this moment.

My job in relation to this book is to be a clear channel for the information that is coming through and to record it accurately. It is important for me to point out here that I was not physically taken over or in any sort of trance when writing this, but I did need to get my thoughts out of the way so the words could come through.

To a large extent my background is unimportant, but if I was reading this I would want to know. It is all part of being able to trust that the information contained here is honest and true. The real test, of course, is how these words feel to you. I believe that for many people they will resonate at a very deep level, as they have done for me. It is important, however, that you have some confidence in the translator, and for that reason I am providing my credentials.

For this type of work, my academic background is probably of less interest than my spiritual one. I have spent most of my working life as an academic at a UK university. Before that, I worked in industry and before that I trained as a bilingual secretary, so translation and secretarial service are not unknown to me. I have a degree in Information Technology and an MA in Teaching and Learning. I am not a scientist in the true sense of the word and my knowledge of physics and chemistry is non-existent. My academic expertise is in Logistics, Supply Chain and Information Systems. With a significant birthday looming on the horizon, I decided to relinquish my full-time university post and become what I prefer to describe as a 'freelancer'. Consequently, there was some spare time: space had been made for this to take place!

My spiritual life is not entirely compatible with my academic one and for the most part I have kept it under wraps at work. Over the years, I have had the pleasure of teaching thousands of students from culturally diverse backgrounds. I have also travelled overseas to teach and I have the utmost respect for everyone I have encountered. It would not have been appropriate to discuss my spiritual beliefs in this context. That is not to say that my spiritual experiences are not important to me. On the contrary, they make me who I am.

My earliest memory is of me lying in my pram and pulling the nose off a much-loved teddy bear. This was well before the time of toy regulation, and in any case this bear was home-made. As a very small infant, I knew who had given the bear to me and that the bear had no feelings, and probably that the nose could be returned to its rightful place, but despite the adult logic, the baby in me cried. I remember being more surprised about my crying than the event which had brought it on. My mother came rushing to find out what the noise was about, and I held up the nose that was still stuck in my little fist. I wanted to tell her that I knew this was an inanimate object with no feelings and I was over-reacting, but as a baby I did not have the words.

During my childhood I experienced feelings that I knew things were going to happen, but these were usually just a few minutes or so before they did and surely everyone did that? I had no brothers or sisters to compare notes with, so everything I did was, I assumed, in some way normal, as it was normal for me. When put to bed, I would sometimes leave my body and travel down the road to my primary school. There was an area behind the stage that fascinated me and I would make regular journeys to check it out. Fortunately, this seems to have been an activity that lasted for a relatively short time. Primary school was not a particularly happy place for me and eventually I had no desire to return there out of hours. One thing that I knew and would tell people was: 'we are not our bodies'. I never had any doubt of that and I remember standing with a group of friends aged around eight saying these words. Children at that time did a lot of name-calling and physical malfunctions were not subject to the political correctness we have today. I couldn't understand the obsession with physical appearance when we were, and are, so much more.

Secondary school was an altogether more pleasant experience. Just having one child, my parents (or rather, my mother) decided that I might do better at a private school. I wasn't performing well in the state system and had what would now be diagnosed as mild dyslexia. The decision about which school to send me to was taken purely on cost grounds. The local stage school was considerably cheaper than the convent school. Thank goodness for that! I fitted in better than I had at primary school, but more importantly, this school gave me some much-needed confidence. The speech and drama lessons, together with acting classes, have given me the voice projection necessary to reach a large group of students who would sometimes prefer to be doing something else. Coincidence? Or it could have been part of a grand plan all along.

Marriage and children followed, life became busy and, for a few years at least, I suppressed the urge to remind people that we are not just our bodies; I think I might be talking to dead people; and by the way, I can remember my past lives (there is so much I could say about this). Suffice to say, I decided to read everything I could about all things 'spiritual' and surrounded myself with crystals and other bits of paraphernalia, which I hoped would help me lift the veil and understand what was going on.

I believe that the spirit world has put me on their own training course, leading me to the next teacher, book or experience. Sometimes this has been less than subtle, such as a book refusing to return to a shelf in a shop and literally falling into my hands, or a chance conversation leading me to just the right teacher at the right time. The culmination of much of this learning process was a 'baptism of light', after which many more things became clear. Learning never ends, of course, and I am sure I shall be trying to improve the quality of messages I can bring through from the spirit world until the moment when I take my last breath and join them myself. Getting accurate messages through to people here is something I take very seriously; it is a massive responsibility and not something that should be undertaken lightly. There are some excellent mediums, but unfortunately also people out there giving messages that are more from themselves than from a contact in the spirit world. For the most part they do not set out to mislead people, but accurate interpretation is everything.

So, what makes me I think I have the right to do this? Despite the potential risk of inaccuracies, I believe that everyone has a right to more information. However, that information must pass through their own personal filter. Does it feel right to you? Does this information enable you to move forward in a more positive way? Will it help to enable you to come to terms with what is an inevitable part of life?

As any student will tell you, my training as an academic means that I would normally write 'academically', using numerous citations to back up every statement and include an extensive reference list. By taking dictation, as described above, it has not been possible to do this and I have resisted the urge to try to cross-reference the information with current scientific thinking. Mostly that would not have been possible anyway but, as I investigated further, there is research that could support what I have been told but owing to my lack of specialist knowledge, I have taken the decision not to do that. If I misinterpreted what I consider to be academic support for one of the concepts given to me, then it might have detracted from the overall message.

It is in my nature to question everything I am doing and to try and improve. So, questions as to the authenticity of what is presented here have been on my mind, too. In the end I had to just 'get out of the way' and let the process unfold. As a seeker of truth, I am hoping that the questions that make me wonder will be of interest to others. Most of all, I just hope to do a really good job!

CHAPTER 1
FIRST MEETING

Prior to the morning of 25 October, I had been asked, 'What do people in the spirit world do all day when they are not waiting around to talk to mediums like you?'. This seemed a very reasonable question to ask and I honestly did not have a clear answer. The question started me thinking about death and made me realise that despite all the spiritual work that I had done, I knew very little.

I believe that it was this question and my subsequent wonderings which prompted this book. Someone somewhere heard my thoughts and decided to give me some answers. When I sat down at the computer on that first morning, I had a fair idea that death would be the topic of the communication.

It must seem strange to many people to be able to 'hear' spirits and the reason that word is highlighted is because many mediums do not hear words with their ears. Occasionally you can, but often the communication makes use of several senses and interpreting messages can sometimes be likened to a game of charades. This communication, however, was quite clear. The person I was talking to might as well have been present in physical form in the same room. Although on that first morning I could not clairvoyantly see them clearly, the words in my head were very clear.

To help with understanding, my words are in italics and indented. The spirit communication is aligned against the left-hand margin and is in slightly bolder type.

And so it begins.

So, you want to know about death? Why?

Because it happens to everyone at some point in their life and it is happening to people every day in many ways.

Has it ever occurred to you that you might not like what you find out? Could there be a very good reason why it is behind the veil?

The people who come back to talk to mediums don't usually appear to be terribly unhappy. They seem to possess a certain clarity that they may not have had on earth. They never say what they have been up to, though, and that is the bit that I am very unclear about. What do they do all day? You can't be hanging around waiting for some random medium to put in a call – what do you do?

Life 'here' (notice I am not saying 'up here') is not too unlike life on earth. It mirrors it.

But, how can it? You leave everything you ever knew.

Well this is one of the concepts we need to explore. You say 'leave' and yet in fact we don't leave at all. We are still here. There is no 'up here' ... just 'here'.

So, what can you see?

We can see you, but so much more. Our perception is expanded from the view on earth. We see (a part of) everything that ever was and ever will be, BUT not all of us and not all at the same time.

Gosh! This is confusing – genuinely.

If you go on holiday somewhere new, your view of it is dependent on the journey getting there, what you were hoping to get out of the holiday, where you choose to stay, who goes with you and what you do while you are there. Not everyone chooses to climb up the tallest mountain for a bird's-eye view. Some people have no interest in doing that and are more than happy to sit or sleep on the beach, go to the bar and dance the night away. It is a bit like that here.

We have a free will, just as you do where you are.

Some people see greater possibilities. Everyone does in the end (and time has a different meaning here, but that is another story). People who were interested in the spirit world whilst on earth are much more likely to take an interest in communicating from this side. If it was something that didn't cross your radar when you were alive, why would you be interested in it now?

It can be true of people who have had a long illness or a difficult life. When they arrive, they just want to rest up and clear their head (yes, I do appreciate the irony of that comment, but it is important to use words that you can relate to – there will be ample time to go into mind, body and spirit, as you like to call it, later).

Everyone is equal. This is an equal opportunity venue! But when people have free will, they decide to use it in different ways. How many times do you see people who (you may think, from your viewpoint) are not making the most of the opportunities presented to them? You might be critical of how they choose to spend their money, or indeed the fact that they do not spend their money to see more of the world, or help others. That is their choice. Whether you agree with their choices or not is of no consequence. They are their choices and they have every right to exercise them. It is the same here.

So, are there are beaches for them to sit on and nightclubs to frequent?
If that is what they want and they choose to spend their time that way, then yes. If that was your idea of heaven (when on earth) then to a large extent that is what you will create when you get a chance to do so. You experience your deepest expectation.

Is that where the concept of hell came from?
This is not the moment to talk about that concept – we can do that later, but suffice to say, if you feel guilty about something and believe that you will be punished then you are in fact creating your own punishment. Rather than finding a beach to sit on, you may create a version of your

deepest fears, if you believe that you deserve to be punished and that is what is waiting for you.

On the other hand, there are people who commit terrible crimes on earth and who do not have a Hell Experience; purely because they do not have the capacity to feel guilty. This may be due to many things, but mainly an inability to experience empathy and compassion. These are the people whom we take under our wing (angelic reference – did you notice that?) and initially curb their free will so that they cannot hurt themselves.

Hurt themselves?

There is no 'physical' here, so they cannot hurt others. Lack of love can only hurt them. To a large extent it is the same on earth, but this is a much bigger concept and one that is even too big for this book; later, maybe.

So how do we create the beach or the nightclub or the beautiful garden to sit in?

People tend to create houses first – that is what you are mostly used to. Somewhere to live.

Do we need somewhere to live?

Not in the sense of shielding you from the elements, but where we live is often an extension of our personality in some way. People often perceive their own value based on where they live. So when given the chance, they tend to stick to what they know. Many people create the same home as the one they have just left, but then later (there is that time issue again, which we need to discuss) they come to the decision that what they had on earth is not right for them and they create something else.

How does this 'creation process' manifest itself?

If someone was a builder, electrician or plumber here, does it mean that is what awaits them there?

The actual creation process does not require any physical effort. Let's get that clear. There is no physical, so how could it?

However, a builder, electrician, plumber or carpenter might decide, for a while at least, that they want to carry on doing that for a while. They might have enjoyed it when on earth, enjoy creating the sensation of physical work, but in fact they are not actually producing anything physical at all. When they realise that, they tend to choose something different.

So, what is required to 'create'? Merely intention?
Yes, that is it. It is a transmutation of the energy field, based on a soul's intention.

How long does it take?
Exactly as long as you expect or intend it to! Although it can happen instantaneously, of course.

Is this how healing works? I often think that when I am doing reiki, or crystal healing as I might call it, all I am in fact doing is using tools that focus my mind and that intention is the key to the process.
Yes, there are certainly simultaneous similarities. Let me explain. The healing is already there. Whether you or the next person or the patient have the intention to create it is by the by. The healing exists in energetic form. The intention opens a pathway (puts the road in, if you like) for it to reach its subject. They could do this themselves, but not knowing what is possible, they feel unable to do it.

Once people have crossed over, this process becomes much clearer as they can see it happening. When in the non-physical, you are more aware of the non-physical energies that surround you. Having said that, some people choose not to look right away. The energies are hidden in plain sight, but that does not mean that everyone sees them if they are not looking.

Doesn't that create some sort of inequality?
Absolutely not! Like I said, this is an equal opportunities venue! When given free will it is just that. You do not have to take an option that

someone else thinks is right for you – the decision is entirely yours and influenced by your soul's journey. You may choose not to look for whatever reason – it is very similar on earth.

I think when people you love die, besides the obvious loss and knowledge that life will never be the same – you want to know that they are alright. That they are in a better place and free from pain and worry. Is there anything you can say that will assure me of that?

To make YOU feel better?

Yes, I suppose so. Especially when children die, or a much-loved partner – you need comfort.

And that is exactly why you are asking me that question. It is for you and not for them.

I disagree. You want them to be happy and if that means you are unhappy, in order for them to be happy, then that is a trade-off. Probably an acceptable one for many people.

So, someone dies and you wish to create a particular misery for yourself so that they can enjoy an afterlife that is full of sunshine and roses?

Well, when you put it like that it seems a bit of an odd thing to say, but I suppose so.

So, you are saying that your free will should impact on theirs?

In a way I suppose I am.

That if you make a trade-off and become a martyr for the cause then they will somehow get some special treatment when they arrive?

Not special treatment – no.

Then what difference would it make whether you are happy or sad?

The ties of love are like strings that attach you to your loved one and remain after death. They don't die with the person; they transmute into a different energy form, but they are very much there. Now imagine that in this equal opportunities venue you see your loved one on earth prostrating themselves on the floor every day, refusing all invitations and generally being miserable in the misapprehension that something they do on earth will impact the type of experience for their loved one in heaven (we will use this word for convenience for now, but will look at the concept later). How will that person feel?

They cannot communicate with you (not readily, anyway). They feel the emotion of your pain through the energy strings that hold you together and the worst thing about it is ... it doesn't make any difference at all.

Whether you are happy or sad affects them in the same way as if it had happened on earth. If they loved you then they would not have wanted to see you suffer (although they know that a process must pass) and if they didn't give a fig when they were alive, why would they necessarily give a fig now?

Where there is no physical there can be no physical pain. So be certain that is the case. Where there was emotional pain (a suicide for example) – some of that may come with them, but they are helped through it. They are not suffering in the traditional sense. They are enlightened. Suicide requires much more discussion, but let's say that emotional pain on earth can often result in physical pain. When the latter is removed, the emotional pain can be lessened and finally transmuted.

Remember that time has a different meaning here, so the time-lag between passing and transmuting the energy that was present when someone took their own life is very short here, but in your terms it might be interpreted differently. For the subject concerned, this happens in the blink of an eye.

So, what you are saying is that they will always be 'alright'?
Yes, in the traditional sense that you are asking that question. It is true to say that people who pass often still have some very strong ties to earth. A grandparent or parent who loved you when they were alive will still love you after they die. The same can be said of a long-term much-loved

partner, of course. They still go on loving and caring.

Consequently, when they see that you are unhappy about their passing, they want to try and get a message back to reassure you that they are doing OK. They will often provide some evidence to demonstrate that they know what you have been doing since their death, just to show that they still care and have been attending family events.

Now I know that this idea can freak people out! The idea that your dead husband is watching you making love to another man will make people feel uncomfortable, or that your mum is watching you in bed with your partner. And let's not even get on to the fact that people worry someone is watching them on toilet!

What about that?

Free will comes in here again, I am afraid. People, whilst living, could potentially snoop on other people in their most private moments. With advances in technology, many more people can set up cameras in their homes and spy on people while they are away. The majority of people choose not to do that. They would deem it inappropriate and not like the way it would make them feel.

On the other hand, social media is making it very easy to share moments with everyone and people have no problem with posting pictures of themselves on the Web. There is a whole different argument about whether these pictures represent real life and their impact on others, but the fact is, people have their private and public moments.

This changes very little when you pass. You know your family and loved ones have their private and public moments. It is OK to share a few of their private moments, when they might be crying, or seeing a baby smile for the first time, but most people would feel uncomfortable watching someone on the toilet.

Everyone makes a judgement call about what is and is not appropriate.

The other point is, given the chance, how much of your time would you spend following someone else around? Would you not want to do your own thing, especially when you can create whatever you want?

That is where I am leaving things today. We will pick this up again tomorrow.

Thank you.

I am still not sure what to call you – I keep thinking of the name Patrick, but it doesn't feel completely right.

That will do for now.

CHAPTER 2
A PROCESS OR A DESTINATION?

THURSDAY 26 OCTOBER 2017

Is death a process or a destination?

Is life a process or a destination?

I agree this is not an easy question to answer. A bit of both, I suppose. We progress from birth to death, but not all progress takes you in a forward motion. Is it like that in heaven?

Like I said previously, the word 'heaven' needs some further definition, but for now we are going to use that word. To some extent it is not a destination – although earth could be described as that. It is more of a home-coming.

A home-coming?

It is your source. So, what else might we call it?

I have seen it written, and many people say, 'we are spiritual souls having an earthly experience'. Is this true?

To some extent but, as you might expect, it is rather more complicated than this.

Can you explain more, please?

Energy essence emanates from this source.

Or rather it did?

Now this is one of the concepts that can be very difficult for you to perceive from your vantage point. Time does not go forward to back. Energy has existed for all time (or at least as far back as it is practical to explain), however it transmutes, so is constantly changing, but that changing happens simultaneously. Although you are there sitting at your computer, your energy essence (or at least the energy essence associated with you) is in many other 'places' at the same time. There is even some of it in me and some of mine in you.

Phew ... can you give me some more examples, please? I don't understand the first thing about quantum physics, but when this sort of thing is discussed, I have heard about polarity and energy splitting. Is it anything to do with this?

Actually no, that is an oversimplification of what goes on, but you could say that the theories of quantum physics are getting much closer to the truth.

What I am saying is that energy is there. It has transmuted many millions of times to make different forms based on its own will. Energy is not there for our command. Energy is life itself.

Is this what people call God?

Again, this is not a discussion that is appropriate here, but suffice it to say that we do not command energy. Energy commands us. However, energy has transmuted to form what we understand as people and things. We are not superior to the energy that created us. We are equal – we are all equal and have come from the same energy source.

So what you are saying is that 'we are all one' – which is something else I have read.

Yes, and we really are all made of energy transmuted in one form or another from the same source; that goes for the computer you are sitting at and the chair you are sitting on. The difference is that the energy has been transmuted for different purposes.

Who decides how or what energy is used for what purpose?

The energy decides.

And we are all energy, so we all decide?

The chair does not suddenly decide to become a desk (although it has the potential to do so). You do not suddenly decide to become a frog (although again, potentially the energy that forms your body most certainly has the potential to take on other life forms).

At this point is seems prudent to discuss body and soul, if only briefly. When you die, you shed your body in the same way you take off a coat. That coat then prepares for the energy contained within it to transmute to something else. So it might be burned, in the case of cremation, or buried. In either or both cases, the energy transforms into something else. Another form of energy. Time in this context has no relevance, so whether that is almost immediate (if a body is cremated) or over a period of years (if buried) is of no consequence.

At the point of death, or at least within a few minutes in your perception, the soul leaves the body. I know you have witnessed this happening yourself when your mother died. What is left is a husk – the personality, soul, essence of that person takes on a different form. It is released from the body and has its freedom!

Could you please just give me a little more explanation about how energy commands us, and yet we are energy.

As you are, where you are, you see everything as separate. You are you, and you have nothing at all to do with not only your friends but your family, too. You all operate quite independently (or at least that is your perception). You might say 'we are one' to a close partner, but if you say that to one of your children, or even a close friend, they will almost certainly disagree.

The fact is, we are much more connected than people think and that goes for every colour and creed. Also for every animal species, and even insects and other very miniscule creatures that play their own important role in your ecosystem. That is not to say that those energy forms are able to communicate with one another at the same level that you can do with your peers. However, there is only one energy source, so if they exist on any level then they can only have been made from the same stuff.

This applies to things you cannot perceive with your five senses on earth. Including those of us who inhabit a different realm. Just because you can't touch it, hear it, see it or feel it – it doesn't mean that the energy is not there. In fact, I can assure you it is very much there!

This is an awful lot to take in. I can understand a little more now about why you asked me if I really wanted to know all this stuff! Personally, I do. It seems to me to be the most important thing in the universe (I was going to say world, but I can see it expands beyond that) to know what is really going on.

There are so many people trying to kill one another. Surely if this was more widely understood then it could make the world a more peaceful place.

People will always follow their prophets and gurus, because people need to feel they are living their lives in the best way. Each prophet offers a version of the perfect life. Which prophet someone follows is often dependent on where in the world they were born and what influences they have been subjected to. There is no one right way.

Even if people believe and accept that we are all from the one source, they will still believe that their prophet offers a better version of Utopia than anyone else's. It is unrealistic to believe that getting a book out like this is going to change the world you live in.

Oh, please believe me, I would never assume I had the power to change anything!

Then why are we doing this? It is important to be clear.

Primarily, because I want to understand. Secondly, because if I want to understand what is going on then I suspect at least a few other people do too, and thirdly, when you lose someone to death it is the most devastating thing. Most people, I believe, are looking for some comfort and assurance that their loved one has gone to a better place.

OK, it is important that you realise what this can be. This is not the first time that we have attempted to get material 'out there' – far from it. Much is never published and what is published is often subjected to ridicule. What we are doing here is transmuting some energy into the written word. We are giving something life. These words then take on an energy of their own. What happens to them will be as the result of the energies that interact with them along the way.

For example, you could delete everything you have written so far. The storage space on your computer will retain the image of the words for a while (the essence of the words); the meaning of our discussions will probably impact on your own energy for a while – you may even tell people about these discussions, thus interacting with their energy; but essentially, the energy that we are creating here and now will lie dormant until your computer crashes (dies) and then the words are combined with the energy taken up by the computer and enter the ether when the computer is burnt or otherwise disposed of.

Alternatively, these words may receive a wider reading and can interact with the energy of a wide range of readers. To some extent this is your choice, as you can choose not to delete our writings and you may decide to send this to a literary agent or post the words on the Internet. Whoever reads the words will mingle their energy with the energy used to create them. As they do so, the energy becomes stronger. Eventually, when you die and have no influence over how the words are posted, they have the potential to take on their own life. As people talk about the words, they become stronger and gather more energy.

Is this why it is important to always express kind and positive thoughts?
Exactly.

Anything said, written or done, or even thought, is 'out there'. If it is positive and kind then the out-there energy is positive and kind. If it is cruel and hurtful then that energy can be cruel and hurtful. Once created, it will need to be transmuted into something else for it to take on a different form.

*You have spoken a lot about 'transmuted energy'. Can you provide
some examples of how energy transmutes, please?*

Certainly. We spoke earlier about intention. What we said was that when
you are doing healing, you create a pathway for the healing to reach the
subject. The healing is already there. The transmutation creates a pathway
for the energy to change form or to reach a positive point for transformation.

This all still sounds very complicated.

Once negative energy (or positive energy even, as this can work equally
well in reverse) is formed … I want to point out here that we are not just
talking about positive and negative – we are talking about everything
that exists. Once whatever it is has been formed, it has the potential to
take on life. That does not mean that the computer and chair that I was
talking about earlier have a soul as such, but they 'take on life'; or rather,
'identity'. Your computer, my chair, etc. The things that happen to my
chair help to identify it. The colour it is painted, the type of fabric on the
seat, the tea I spilt on it. My chair can have an identity that is different
from your chair, even if hundreds or even thousands of the same type of
chair were made at the same time. As those chairs go through their useful
lives, energies interact with them and intertwine with them. If someone
sat on that chair every day of their life, then the chair would certainly
pick up a great deal of the energy of that person. For sensitive people, that
means they could pick up information about the person who sat in it for a
prolonged amount of time, as they can 'read' the energy of the chair.

This is how psychometry works, then?

Yes, energy is fluid and it interacts. It is unlimited, so it is not weakened
by the interaction: if anything, the interaction makes it stronger, as
it absorbs energy from the subject or situations surrounding it and
expands because of it.

This means, then, that energy in all forms can be extremely powerful.
If something is perceived as 'negative' – and let us be clear that what one

person might perceive as negative, another believes to be 'transformative – if a sufficient amount of energy is produced that wants change, then a pathway can be created that will enable other energies which are on a different frequency to interact with it and make that change happen.

A clear, everyday example, please?

You place a pan of oil on a hob and it catches fire. For most people that would be a change of energy that would not be considered desirable as it has the potential to change everything around it with further negative consequences. The energy of the fire has a particular form and a strong one at that. If you throw a damp cloth over the pan at this point, you are interacting with the energy of the fire. You are transmuting that energy by turning it into something else and, in this scenario, something more desirable. By interacting with the energy, you have created a pathway to enable the energy to transmute into something that ensures that your house remains intact.

If you decide to leave the pan on the hob and it continues to burn, the energy of the fire will gather further momentum. You will have then created a pathway to transmute even more energy into a different (less desirable) form.

Did I detect a joke?

You may well have done! Although the scenario I have quoted has nothing amusing about it.

Of course!

You asked for an everyday example and that is what you got. This sort of scenario happens every day to someone.

End of session for today.

CHAPTER 3
ASKING FOR PROOF

The previous day, I had asked for someone to contact me who could tell me what a typical day in heaven was like. For a while, I believed I was talking to someone I had once known in life – a much-loved uncle who shared my interest in otherworldly things. However, there was something about this conversation that did not feel quite right to me and for this reason I have decided to omit it. I think it was given to me as a reminder to remain discerning about the information I was being given, but it did unsettle me and I started to question everything. I approached the following session asking for proof.

TUESDAY 31 OCTOBER 2017

I am not sure what happened yesterday.

Having some evidence that what we are doing is right, true and honest is extremely important to me. From this view-point on earth, it is very difficult to tell what is right and where information is coming from. The only way to do that (and give me confidence that I am not misleading people and doing something dishonest) is if I am given something that I can verify.

The problem with yesterday was twofold. First of all, I started to question if I was really talking to the person I thought I was, because the person I knew would not have misquoted something when he was here and secondly, I started to question everything, because it made me think that I might only be bringing through information that I already know in my logical mind.

I am just trying to record, accurately, what I am being told from the afterlife about what it is like to exist there.

Did it feel different to what I was dictating last week?

Well yes, it felt as though it could be from the earthly me, but how can I be sure that what I am hearing is not coming from another part of me?

What might that be?

My subconscious.

OK, and how is your subconscious different to your soul?

I have no idea! I just know that I need some concrete proof about something I cannot ...

What? Hear? See? Feel? – I thought you did that anyway when giving readings?

Yes, but it is very difficult to distinguish sometimes what is imagination and what is message!

I honestly believe that getting information from the afterlife is essential. People are burying their heads in the sand.

And what is wrong with that? Why do they need to know?

Because it can give people comfort.

Then does it matter if it is true?

Why not give them a nice story – something to help them sleep at night? That approach has worked for centuries. Why is the truth so important now? And let us remember here that truth can have many versions and interpretations.

I just want to give a representation of what people do all day in heaven.

And did you not get a feel for that yesterday?

Yes, but how do I know that what happened yesterday was not my hopes and wishes for what happens? Maybe I have some memories of things that happened between lives and I am just recounting those.

And that would be a problem how?

You are trying to control the process, which you cannot. You can be a

part of the process, but you cannot control it.

Well, my free will requests proof.

Do you want to stop here?

Absolutely not!!!!!!!!!!!!! I want to learn how I can do this better. And by 'better', I mean make sure that the information I am bringing through is the best that it can possibly be.

You are doing OK for now. There will be some editing at the end and I have told you that already.

Is there any way that you can provide something more concrete for me to go on, please?

Picture this. You and lots of other people live in a room, at the end of which is a very large door. After 70 or more years, the door opens and either one or a few people go through the door and it closes very quickly afterwards. You wonder probably daily what is on the other side of the door, but there are chores to be done and people to talk to in the room, and you only really think about the door when someone you know goes through it – or when you think you might be next!

No one ever comes back through that door. Occasionally, you hear what you think are words coming from the other side of the door. But you can't really be sure, as there is a lot of noise in the room you are in. Sometimes you put your ear to the door to see if you can hear more. You might even put a glass to the wall to see if you can hear anything through that, and you know someone who once tried to listen with some specialist audio equipment. The fact of the matter is that once someone goes through that door, their life on the other side is a complete mystery.

What do you do?

You have various options. You can forget all about the door and live your life as though it did not exist (and many people choose to do this), or you can spend your life trying to work out what awaits you. The first option means that, for the most part, you enjoy your life in the room you are in. The second option means that you are in constant state of worry or wonder about what might lie on the other side and the only time that you will find out is when you go through the door yourself. On the day that happens, you might be very disappointed! There could be nothing at all – just blackness. And you will have wasted the life that you had, pondering about absolutely nothing. Some might say that is an absolute waste, when you could have been off enjoying yourself.

On the other hand, life the other side of the door could be a mirror image of life on the previous side. When you have been in the second room for a while, your memory of the first room starts to fade and you get curious about Room 1. What really happened when I lived there? Did I imagine everything? Can I get back?

This is a human condition. Always looking for the next door, the next experience and next death, and not fully engaging with the one you are in.

Do you think that is what I am doing?

Not exactly, but some people are very happy ignoring the door. For the majority of people, there is not a massive need to know what there is on the other side.

You are trying to satisfy the curiosity of the smaller number of people who are looking for something more than what is on offer at the time.

But surely, going back to this door, if that door had been left open for longer, or if people could travel between the two rooms, then the mystery would be gone and they could choose where to live?

Are you proposing then that people can do that on earth? The only way to travel through that door is through birth or death. It is not a holiday destination!

You are making a big assumption that people want to know, and that 'knowing' is desirable and will improve their lives on earth. It could have the completely opposite effect: when life on earth gets even a little bit tough, they decide that they will kill themselves and start again on the other side. You have created such a lovely cosy picture of somewhere they can do whatever they like, when they like and have everything they want at 'the touch of a creative button', so why would anyone not want to go?

So you are saying that I should not create such a rosy picture?

I am saying that you must be responsible for what you create.

If the details remain a little fuzzy, you are giving people the option to decide whether they want to open that door and peek inside. If they do, and they like what they see, you are giving them the option to tell themselves that it is all a dream and that what you have described probably does not exist. They return to their lives and choose not to think about the door again for a long while, and concentrate on what they need and want to do on earth.

Do you get my point?

Yes, I do. But as the person transcribing this, doesn't this give me a few more rights than someone else?

Why should it? I have told you many times that this is an equal opportunity venue!

But people reading this will think this is a massive cop-out on my part.

Does that matter?

To me, yes, it does. I identify myself as being an honest person and someone who tells the truth as I see it.

And isn't that what you are doing?

Yes, but I might not be being honest with myself about where this information is coming from. I don't mind at all devoting my time to this and I am grateful, very grateful, for the opportunity to do it. Even if I only show this to a couple of people, I am putting myself right out there and saying that this book represents who I am. With anything spiritual that is a risk, but if you know in your heart that what you produce is the best that you could possibly do, and as honest and accurate as you can possibly make it, then you don't mind putting your neck on the block.

Can you suggest anything that might help me in my dilemma, please?

Yes. That you devote the time to do what you have promised and not question the content at this stage. That you record, to the best of your ability, what is presented to you and that you acknowledge that there is a polarity to everything that you produce. A knife can cut your food to enable you to eat, but it can also kill a child. There is a responsibility that comes with owning a knife. On the other hand, if someone had said many eons ago, 'no knives, because they are far too dangerous' then society would not have got as far as it has. But the person making that first knife needs to understand that once realised, the energy of the knife has the power to work for good or evil.

I didn't think there was supposed to be evil in heaven.

You are not in heaven! You are releasing this energy on earth and there are consequences. You need to wield the knife very carefully and you may not understand what it can do yet. You just want it to cut food, but it has many other uses and not all of them are positive.

So basically, you are just saying – turn up, do your stuff and stop asking questions?

Stop asking questions about the validity of what you are doing at this stage, as you cannot see the big picture now.

I would just like to make one request though, please: throughout this project, and particularly in the early stages, can you please give me some signs, and some obvious ones at that? Just to let me know that other entities are involved in doing this and that everything I am writing is not coming from my over-active imagination*.

I will see what I can do.

This is enough for today.

Since writing these lines, four years have passed and I have been presented with many different entities that have given me a great deal of further information. Although I was understandably sceptical at the start, I have embraced the 'turn up, do your stuff and stop asking questions' philosophy. I still use my discernment and not everything will make publication.

One of the major issues for me with this book is that any positive interpretation of the afterlife carries with it a great deal of responsibility: not only on my part as the writer, but also on your part as the reader. We are spiritual souls having an earthly experience. We are here for a reason and there are things we pre-determined that we want to achieve.

However idyllic the afterlife may appear to be, the message is very clear. This is where we are supposed to be, and however uncomfortable and unhappy we may be at certain points in our lives, it is not for us from our earthly vantage point to decide when to leave to go home. That then becomes mission aborted and not mission accomplished, and any lessons we have not learned in this life will be presented again.

If there is anything in this book that leads you to want to end your life prematurely, I urge you to seek help immediately. It is not your destiny and it is not the plan for you. You are not alone and you are loved. The Samaritans can be contacted on 116 123, or email jo@samaritans.org

CHAPTER 4
'BATTRICK'

My insistence on being provided with proof did not subside immediately. The session on 1 November started a little later than normal, as we had a guest staying over and I wasn't prepared to explain my new job at this stage.

WEDNESDAY 1 NOVEMBER 2017

Who are you, Patrick?
Firstly, my name is not Patrick, but that is what you seem to want to call me.
What is your name?
Batrik
I have never heard of this name.
Just because you have not heard of it does not mean the name is incorrect!
Anyway, it isn't spelt correctly:
BATTRICK
(I 'Googled' the name.)
This is an old English surname.
It is also my name.
So, who are you?
I am the person talking to you!
Who were you?
Are you real?
As real as you are.
Battrick, I would very much like to work successfully with you and it helps to know who I am talking to.

What do you want to know?

Have you ever lived on earth?

Yes, many times.

What was your earliest life?

In non-human form, many millennia ago.

When was your latest life?

During the English Civil War.

Which side were you on?

Neither!

I hated war then, as I do now. It is a pointless expression of greed and power. There are no winners and the victors are losers, too.

There will always be loss of life on both sides.

What was your name during the Civil War?

It was Battrick, which is why I am giving you that name now. I have many names, but that is one you should be able to relate to.

OK. Where in the country did you live?

Birmingham.

Birmingham?

Surely that hardly existed then?

It existed alright. Mainly farmland, but there was a strong community of Oliver Cromwell supporters. They were craftspeople. I was a craftsperson.

What exactly did you make?

Anything and everything that was needed. Gates, doors, wheels, bolts in iron, you name it and I made it.

What happened to you in that life?

Our village was torn apart. Neighbour against neighbour. I refused to fight, so I was killed by my own people.

Were you married?

I had a 'wife', but not in the official sense. She was expecting our first child and was left all alone.

You sound very bitter about all this. Not very heavenly!

I was very bitter at the time, but people act out of character when they are motivated by creed and greed. When they perceive a threat from others – from outside. Their fear makes them act in this way and their ignorance fuels it.

So, you haven't returned to earth?

No – would you wish to return to that sort of lie?

I am very sorry to hear this.

So, what have you done since?

Everything I can to promote understanding and kindness.

So that is why you are helping me now?

You could say that.

Is there anywhere left in modern Birmingham that would have been around when you were there?

Very little.

I lived to the west of the town, out in the countryside. Three miles from the centre.

(I took time out to check the information given: Birmingham did indeed support the parliamentarians during the Civil War and there was a major battle, The Battle of Birmingham.

What Battrick describes is quite feasible … and very sad.

The area he lived in seems to have been swallowed up in the general conurbation that is Birmingham, but as far as I can tell it would have been around what is now Harborne.

I get the impression we are done for the day.)

CHAPTER 5
EXISTENTIALISM

After sitting at the computer for a few seconds, the following word came to me:

'Existentialism'

I was having a great deal of difficulty spelling the word and had no idea what it meant, so I had to look it up.

Existentialism (noun): 'A doctrine that concentrates on the existence of the individual, who, being free and responsible, is held to be what he makes himself by the self-development of his essence through acts of will' (*Oxford English Dictionary*)

I am sorry it took me so long to spell it, but now I can see it is very relevant.

Where do we start?

The meaning of life is determined by the life. Or rather that energy blob that has given life to an individual.

There are so many questions associated with that sentence, but I will gloss over that now because I sense we are talking about something else.

Yes. If we are saying that the meaning of life is a sub energy that has been created by an individual energy – where does that leave us?

Confused.

Indeed, but that is in a way what is happening here. Energy creates events that are predetermined, to the extent that the mind/soul has requested them on one level or another. That same energy, or the energy of associated individuals, can/will interact with the created energetic

event. There is a further energy that is created based on the reaction of the individual energy that interacts with it.

A collection of energetic events and/or the reaction of the associated individual energies result in a theory about life, and the soul/mind energies associate deeper meaning, which they understand as theory. After a while, the events perform to fit the theory and provide reinforcement for the individual.

But what is actually happening – is this all about just perception?
No, on the contrary, this is about individuals determining their future based on microcosm events, creating their own 'theories' about what should happen next and the energy (which always follows the intention) obliges by creating more and more events that fit the theory.

Where there is a tipping point of matter that does not agree with the original theory, there is the potential for further change. Those individual energies then subconsciously or consciously create events which match the theories they believe in.

If their belief is strong enough and if there are a sufficient (tipping point) number of energies which perceive an alternative theory, then doubt sets in about the original theory and change can happen. This can take time or it can happen very quickly; millennia or minutes.

I think I am just about following the theory – probably because on some level I want to believe it!
Yes, and because you have read books telling you that you create your own future and so this theory fits in with this.

Phew, this is an awful lot to take in. To what extent does this happen on an individual level and at a world level? I mean, can my optimism for example affect my personal future, because I tend to 'look on the bright side', or can .... to be honest I don't know what I mean. Can you give some clear example, please?
There is a person (man) on a boat out at sea. The sea looks choppy, but

this person has been out in weather like this before and he has not had a major problem before. He has his reasons for wanting to go out in the boat. The deep-sea fish that sometimes you cannot catch come nearer the surface before a storm and this is a good opportunity to make some money. The man is trying to buy his wife her own boat and he has almost enough money to get that if he can just have a few good outings in the one boat he has.

The coast-guard is giving a poor weather warning, but not a severe one. The fisherman knows how long it takes him to bring the catch home – this method has worked many times before. From when the sky looks a certain way there are normally three and a half hours before things get tough. A successful fishing trip can happen in two and a half hours. This is his livelihood and he cannot afford to sit at home every time it gets a little bit dark and overcast. There is a risk, but it is a measured one, based on his past experience.

His wife is much more cautious. She would rather buy a van than a boat, so that she can sell the vegetables she grows at the market. She would rather be in a field than on the sea, but her husband insists that it will only be for a few years and then they will have enough money to buy a nicer house and have the children she so dearly wants.

The overall dream is the same but there are two ways to achieve it.

On this particular day, the wife is working in the field and knows that her husband is about to get into his boat. She loves him dearly, as he does her, and their energy fields are very much intertwined. It doesn't matter whether they are standing together or are miles apart. The physicality of the interaction of the energy plays no part. Her love/intention/interest in her partner is enough to create that interaction, so her thoughts are just as powerful as if she was actually standing with him in the boat.

As she looks up to the sky, she notices that the clouds look a tiny bit darker than usual. She knows the danger of the sea, as she lost her father and brother that way. She starts to worry.

There are other people on the sea, in the field, on the beach, in aircraft, etc. that have a vested interest in the weather on this day. They may not know each other, but they all have an interaction with the energy that creates the weather.

The man in the boat today decides it is worth going ahead. He has a very slightly uneasy feeling, which is probably due to the interaction of energy from his loving wife. He has been out at sea for 45 minutes when a wave comes up from nowhere and knocks him off course. He takes this a little more seriously than he might have done, as it has added to that uneasy feeling. He checks the weather forecast, which is still saying 'poor', rather than severe. What does he do? Does he play it safe and return home, at risk (he believes) of disappointing his wife because he has not earned any money this day, or does he carry on and 'be a man', because if he turns back he will probably sail into harbour amidst calm seas and blue skies. This is his dilemma.

It is fuelled, too, by what he thinks his wife wants (which in this case may not be correct) and his perceptions about himself (that he may not be 'man' enough), and also what he fears people may think of him and how that interacts with his perception of himself as he returns to shore.

The severity of these thoughts, and how many times they have occurred before, will determine his decision either to carry on or return to shore.

The severity of the weather on that day is not dependent on the thoughts or intentions of one or two people. The weather on that day has been determined by the thoughts and actions of many people over time. In other words, the severity of that particular storm on that day is already determined and had been for a good while before the man actually set sail. He, however, has free will (although it may not feel like that to him) as to how he reacts.

If he decides to carry on, there is a chance, given the severity of the storm, that he may not return at all to his loving wife. She will not have a husband, the children she so dearly wanted or the home of her own. As her father and brother are also dead, she will live at the mercy of kind friends. Her self-worth will plummet and she may inadvertently make choices that lead to her early death.

(Could she not meet someone lovely who will take care of her as well?)
Yes, of course, if she in any way sees this as a possibility.

Another scenario is that her husband loses his boat, but the coastguard picks him up and brings him safely to shore. The experience of that day could affect the fisherman in several ways: he might decide that the sea is not for him and that he will help his wife on the land; he could decide that he will borrow money to buy a new boat and that their dreams will have to be put on hold, or the insurance company could buy him a brand-new boat that is safer and more reliable than the other one.

If he turns back there will be consequences there, too: is he losing his nerve, is he enjoying the sea as much as he used to, etc., etc. ... the possibilities about how he reacts to those thoughts are endless.

What happens?
In this example, it really doesn't matter. The fisherman will make what feels to him like a split-second decision either to return or to carry on. That decision will be because of the thoughts he has had for the best part of his life. It will be influenced by the people he has known, by how many have lost their lives at sea and/or the number of times people have survived storms. It will also depend on his experience about how useful these weather conditions are in catching a bumper load of fish!

He has free will.

He can choose how he reacts to events

The events he experiences are based on his 'theories' about what is possible and what is not.

If almost everyone he knew had met with an accident at sea when it was anything less than calm, or if fish were never caught in these conditions, then his theory would be that it was very unwise to set sail when there was any chance of a storm. His theory would change.

As it is, he has been brought up with stories of brave men battling adverse weather conditions. He can see how people loved the stories and the storytellers became celebrities. He looks up to these people and believes that is the sort of person he should be, someone whom his wife wants him to be.

Regardless of the fisherman, people on earth lead their lives creating these theories. Those theories have their own energy and their own life. Unless there are events which challenge the theory, that is how things remain.

At certain times it is easier to challenge existing theory than at others. People many miles apart can have similar thoughts. They might only be small pebbles in a pond where they are geographically placed, but if people around the world are having similar thoughts then those ideas meet up in the ether and become stronger. When you have lots of small pebbles in lots of ponds that are all interconnected, there is a possibility to challenge the existing theory.

As we said, physicality and geographical positioning make absolutely no difference at all! Ideas matter, as they gradually become energy blobs which can meet up and get stronger. It doesn't matter where you live, or even if you express your thoughts. There is no need to put these ideas in a blog or in a book. From an energy perspective that makes little difference, although it can be argued that as people read your thoughts you have the potential to interact with their energy field and the energy 'blob' becomes bigger.

Please explain what you are referring to as an 'energy blob'.

I am trying to use words you can relate to, but I am using the word 'blob' to indicate that this is not a perfect ball of energy. It can be any shape in your understanding – it can stretch through time and space in order to gather more dust that is magnetically drawn to it based on its thought perspective.

Its thought perspective?

Yes, the energy blob has what you might refer to as a personality type. Like attracts like, so similar personality types enjoy hanging out together. It is the same with this. As the energy blob travels through time and space it gathers factors, theories, ideas, random thoughts, etc. which match its personality.

What about the TIME and space bit?

Yes, I thought you would pick up on that. Remember, time is not linear, so whether these thoughts existed hundreds or even thousands of years ago makes no difference: no physicality – remember?

(At this point I can feel the connection waning a bit – I took a phone call in the middle of this, not ideal!

I get the impression we are done for today. It seems quite exhausting for Battrick to maintain the connection for a long period of time. One and a half hours' dictation seems about right.)

CHAPTER 6
PAIN AND ILLNESS

(There has been a break of one week, owing to a virus that I picked up. I felt too poorly to concentrate and I am hoping that Battrick has understood and will join me today.)

Are you there?

Yes, I am here.

Did you get the message that I would not be around?

Your father told me that he thought you wouldn't make it.

Thanks, Dad!

What are you going to tell me about today?

It might be appropriate to talk about why we get illnesses in the first place.

When you say 'we', do you mean 'we on earth' or is illness in the spirit world, too?

I thought you might ask that.

No physical means that antibodies are not needed to fight infection. However, people can create the effects of illness in order to achieve a goal, but that is true on earth as well as here.

Firstly, why would they do that and secondly, what does that achieve?

Some people identify with illness. They may have been treated more favourably in life when they were ill. Or at least, that may have been their impression. This thought can go back to a busy mother paying a child attention when they were ill. Years ago (as sometimes now), a sick child could mean that a child is not long for this/your world. If they want attention, they might create the same symptoms as their illness, believing this will achieve their goal. Once past childhood, illness might have meant that they did not have to work, or at least not so hard. They may not even have realised what they were doing.

The illness then lasts as long as it is needed and the subject understands that they have a choice in the matter.

Is it like this on earth? Do/did I have a choice about getting sick?

You had a choice about the severity of it and you surrendered to it more than if you had been working, but in doing so you have shortened it. Is that a bad thing? Not necessarily. You made a choice to increase the severity to lessen the time.

I suppose on some level I was thinking along those lines. You must 'battle on' when you are at work, but then it seems to go on for weeks. I thought taking it easier would help my body get over it.

To some extent this was correct.

What should I have done?

Exactly what you chose to do. You are living a physical existence and the physical body needs to be maintained. Not every illness – minor or major – is 'God-given'. Everything has been created and is 'out there'. This means that it has its own will, to a limited extent. Everyone who has interacted with it has had the capacity to mutate it to some degree. Your virus has been around for a while and many people have made an impression on it. It is essentially everywhere in a busy public place. Your body was in fact looking for it! You thought – crowded place – lots of people – probably not as clean as it should be – especially non-wipeable surfaces – if I put my hand on anything and then into my mouth, I shall become ill. You sent out this message loud and clear, so your body and the virus combined to make that happen.

What should I have done?

You could have set up a protection around yourself, by visualising a protective bubble around you and believing that any germs could not get into your system.

Does that work?

It depends how much you truly believe in it and the nature of the various viruses around, and whether you have decided at a subconscious level that 'it is your time to catch something', or any one of a million other random thoughts that you may have had about illness. But yes, that can and does work!

What about more serious illness: what is 'God-given'?

It can be that people before they incarnate believe that their overall mission will be reinforced by planning a life-changing event in advance. They have free will, so they have an opportunity to change that programming if they want to, but sometimes it is the best way to achieve a certain aim.

Can you give me an example, please?

The fisherman in an earlier example may be a very talented artist. He is working in an environment where he is expected to spend all his days fishing. Everyone in the village does the same. It is the only way to make a living and any ideas about producing artwork would be frowned upon. If he became ill – either through a viral infection that left permanent damage or through an accident that left him without his legs, for example, he would not be able to take to his boat to fish. In such circumstances – either through necessity or just to pass the time – he might return to thoughts of art. He could then have a happy life painting and drawing, and might even sell some of his work to fund his life. It could be that making a life-changing event part of his experience would be the only thing that would bring this event about. He would have had the opportunities in his life to do other things, but he might have missed those or decided not to do them, for whatever reason. He therefore programmed the loss of his legs as a way to ensure that his life eventually went to another pattern. He must have had his reasons for doing this.

What could those reasons possibly be to make someone take such a drastic action?

It all depends what his soul's journey wanted to do.

Please explain.

Equal opportunities! Sometimes we don't always use our free will to the best effect. Our souls are influenced by every life event we have ever experienced over millennia. We have a view of ourselves, based on those experiences and how we handled them. It is rather like building a jigsaw puzzle, but without a picture on the box. Free will can be used in many ways. Not all of it for the good of everyone.

But surely in heaven everyone acts nicely towards one another?

I am sorry to shatter your illusions, but not all learning is done on earth! We have greater vision here and that means that the consequences of our actions can be seen immediately and well into the future. It is also possible to change what you have chosen in order to change the outcome of the events and that is the advantage that we have over you.

Unfortunately, and this happens in a limited sense, as individuals here have much more control over what happens to them personally, people still retain a sense of their own power when they pass over. They sometimes take a while to see what their choices have done and then they must decide to take a different course of action.

As we have said before, time has a different meaning here. We see past, present, future, alternative pasts, presents and futures, all in the blink of an eye.

Imagine standing in the centre of a very large sphere. You can travel in any direction and will experience something different each time you do.

Can you get back to the centre of the sphere any time you want?

Not as such. YOU are the centre of the sphere and each time you take a step, you change everything that surrounds you to some degree. If you have free will, and we all do, then you must use it wisely. Your choices have consequences and that is true whether you are there or here.

Gosh, once again it is a lot to take in!

People are influenced by their experiences and if those experiences have been limiting over several lifetimes, it takes them a while to realise all the possibilities open to them.

There is a similar situation on earth, though – wouldn't you agree?

Yes, I suppose families that don't rate education so highly might not encourage their children to go to university. Or a child might look round at his or her peers and not know anyone who stayed at school past 16, and may not consider anything different for themselves, or believe that the pattern can be changed.

Within their circle, any ideas might be quickly deflated as being unrealistic and far too costly. They may of course be airing very real obstacles and making a change when you cannot see viable alternatives – especially if you are a lone voice – is extremely difficult. There are options, but it would be easy to perceive that there are very few.

I suppose this is the reason why so many people buy lottery tickets?

Yes, and winning the lottery is a life-changing event that some people have chosen to build into their experience. The rest may not have seen it as an option before they reincarnated, and of course the number of lottery winners is limited in a lifetime anyway.

What can people do if they want to effect positive change in their lives?

Firstly, they need to be willing to see what they like and don't like about their current experience. This needs to be a very detailed examination. It is not sufficient to say 'I don't like person x or house b'. They need to think about exactly what they do not like about those people or places.

The answer may not be about walking away! It could be about

communicating about problems and working them through. This then becomes a learning experience. If not, the subject may well choose the same thing again.

Thank you for coming back! I am looking forward to doing this again.

WEDNESDAY 29 NOVEMBER 2017

I had to start this session with an apology to Battrick. I wasn't available the previous morning, as I should have been. I was in pain with my back and rather worried about a few things, and I think the whole thing just took over.

I am sorry but I sort of thought that you would have either known in advance or have got the message.

(I am sitting here today with no idea if he will show and if he does – if he will be cross with me. I am worried there is a danger he will not show ever again.)

Battrick – are you there?

I am indeed! I did have some advance warning of yesterday's events and I want to remind you (as a telling-off will make you feel better) that you have made a commitment. On the other hand, this is not a trial! This is an information exchange that should not be stressful, so keep that in mind, although it is necessary to set some boundaries, otherwise the project will not be finished and I cannot wait around for the whole of your life just in case you decide to show up to finish it. Have I made myself clear?

Yes, thank you. What are we going to discuss today?

Well, as you are in some pain then that seems to be a good topic for discussion.

Do you have pain in the afterlife – I sort of assumed not?

People who pass over often need to replicate previous conditions if these are built into their identity. Once here they can quickly shed the pain, but it is within their free choice to do so. There is no physical body, so how can there be physical pain? However, the soul may replicate the pain for a particular purpose, until that pain is no longer required.

How does someone in the spirit world 'shed the pain'?

By choosing to do so. They need at first to recognise that they have created an illusion of pain that is not centred in a physical body. For most people this does not take very long. But if you have spent most of your life in pain whilst in a physical body, it can take a while to realise that it is not part of you. If pain was transient at death then people do not generally identify with it, and at the moment of death it is automatically released.

I would have thought it would all have been?

It can be if the soul has no further use for it!

Who would have use for pain?

Quite a few people find pain (or their ability to cope with it) to be part of their soul's identity. If it is removed too suddenly then they have a loss of identity and that can be a problem when they pass over.

Why?

Leaving one realm and passing into another can be a stressful experience for some people. They may not have been expecting death, even if they had been ill for a long time. A period of adjustment is necessary.

It just seems awful to think that not all pain disappears at death.

But it can if you want it to! Remember – equal opportunities and free will! It is just that people do not always use their free will in the way you expect. Also, some people do not immediately understand that they even have free will.

OK, so what can we do about physical pain on earth?

Let us first be clear, this is not a fairy story. Not all physical pain can be removed on the physical plane. It is unrealistic to think it can be. However, there are things that can be done to eliminate pain for many and reduce it for others.

The strain of a physical muscle will take time to heal. The pain has a purpose to serve in this sense, as it is a warning that your body has its limitations and tolerances, and you may have exceeded both. Your body is a vessel for the soul and you need to respect it as much as possible. So, pain in this instance acts as a warning and has a relationship to how reckless or ill-advised a particular action may have been.

There are sometimes just accidents – plain and simple. You may be responsible for the action that preceded the pain or you may not. If you were, and it could have been avoided, then you learn for next time. If not, it may be that you are helping to provide a lesson for another person about how their actions can cause harm.

Issues can sometimes be more complicated. Sometimes people decide to experience pain at certain times of their lives, as they wish to be reminded about something. This could be to change their lives in a particular way, if they have strayed too far from their original course. A painful illness is very good at focusing the mind on what you really want to do with the rest of your life.

Then there is this whole issue of identity. Pain and illness can provide people with a great deal of attention. Look at me! I am ill! Please give me some attention ... please! Do not take me for granted! I may not be long for this world. If this pain attention syndrome is reinforced, then pain can be a good way to get attention, if you need it. BUT let us make this very clear! Not everyone who has long-term pain is clamouring for attention! On the contrary, they would take many years off their lives just to be pain-free for one hour!

So, the whole pain issue is incredibly complicated.

It can be a reminder; a warning and a lesson; it can be a pre-ordained state, in order to act as a wake-up call for the person in pain, or someone else; it can be brought about to achieve a particular outcome in others.

There is also a situation when people have decided to punish themselves, for whatever reason. They may have decided that some past action (in the current life or a past life) needs some punishment. Just the act of accepting punishment can be healing to the subject and bring about a 'mental balancing of the books'.

There is no entity in the afterlife who demands such a sacrifice – otherwise there would not be free will! This is something that the individual subjects demand of themselves. Their perception of their misdemeanour may far outweigh the original deed. But if their perception demands a life of sacrifice to pain and that is what they have set up for themselves then that is what happens.

So is this what people mean by karma?

In a sense yes, but all karma is self-inflicted. There is no spiritual entity demanding punishment in this world or the next. We judge ourselves, for if we didn't, how would we progress?

So what you are saying is that if I killed someone in a past life, I might have decided to punish myself in this one?

Yes. That punishment may be transient pain at a key point in your earthly life, or it could be a whole life of pain.

And of course, people do not always choose to punish themselves with pain! There are many things that they could plan in their earthly lives in order to balance those mental books! It could be always turning away potentially successful relationships, to ensure a solitary life. It could be a mental illness that prevents them from achieving their potential.

The subjects have their reasons for doing this. It might be that they want to experience a different sort of life, which will help their soul's progression. The reasons are endless.

It should be noted that even though some of these decisions to experience pain of whatever sort may have been made before birth, there is free will on earth and in many cases the opportunity to pick something else might be available.

So, having decided you wanted a solitary life, you may have realised that this is not necessary for your soul's growth and make a new decision to stop pushing people away and enjoy company, and even have a family of your own.

We learn both here and there. We never stop learning, as that is our progression.

OK, progression implies a forward motion and an improvement over time. You said that it wasn't quite like that.

Yes, and that is true, but we have to keep the whole time conversation for another day. Today this is all about pain.

OK, well, I am sitting here at this computer with lots of work to do after I have spoken to you and I am in pain! I would very much like the pain to go away. In fact, I can't wait for it to go away. I can't quite identify with any of the scenarios that you have presented to me.

... Although, I can see that maybe I use illness as a way to avoid work?

Yes, I would have thought so, too! You certainly used that yesterday when you missed our meeting. You had decided not to punish yourself, but you felt guilty and you felt better when you had been very mildly reprimanded. The books were balanced.

You make yourself – or rather you have started to make yourself – more susceptible to illness of various sorts, in order to provide space in your life to do something other than work. You believe on a very deep level that you should work. You owe it to yourself and to other people. At this point in your life, you could survive on one level or another by not working, but you have got it into your head that you must work under any circumstances. BUT at the same time, you are aware of the passing of time in your dimension and you have a desire to do other things. You seem to know that you may not have any more lifetimes on this planet and you rather like the place. You want to enjoy what it has to offer and you prefer not to have to think about work at all. Although this statement is quite complex, as your work ethic is so deeply seated that you can only feel fulfilled by engaging in meaningful work.

So, to get a break, and to remind yourself that you did in fact intend to do other things at this point in your life, you decrease your scepticism in relation to illness and, in this case, pain.

Both give you a reason to stop work! And the desire to stop work is greater than your desire to remove the illness and pain.

Having recognised this, what do I do about it?

Whatever you like! You have free will.

OK. Please talk me through this. I have things I need to do today, as I have committed to them and need to get on with them.

Yes, you have committed to them and now (owing to your work ethic and your desire not to disappoint) you have created this commitment. It makes you feel valued and useful. That is why you did it.

So, having done that, why are you trying to create that illness now and change everything?

Because I am still not thinking about what I really want?

Because in this case, you are not recognising how important it is to you to feel valued and useful. Imagine a long stick. At one end you have the total freedom of absolutely nothing to do – endless days of doing just as you want, no one makes any demands on your time at all, every day is free.

Actually, that sounds a bit boring to me!

At the other end of the stick you have regular work. But this work requires frequent and constant effort. At times it can be thankless (it makes you feel unvalued) and it is often exhausting. Once involved in it, there is little time for anything else.

So you give yourself breaks by inviting your body to get ill, to give you a rest.

As you have got older, the body is getting more tired and has more difficulty in seeing the value, so you create more illness to give you frequent time off.

What can I do?

You have to decide where on that stick you want to put a marker. You have to decide exactly how much work you want, balanced against the lack of anything to do. Putting that mark on the stick can be a very complex and difficult process. Easy enough to make a mark, but how do you know that you are putting it in the right place? The ideas that you hold may, in some cases, go back millennia. They do not unravel overnight. You are a product of all your past experiences. Things happened to you that you did not fully understand at the time. Now that many thousands of earth years may have passed – how do you understand them now? Not all your lives were even on earth and you are shaped by experiences in the afterlife, as well.

Putting down that mark and exercising your free will in a way that is most beneficial to your soul's growth is extremely complex.

Needless to say, many people do not always get this right and swing around on that stick.

Let me explain. If you have a stick or pole and you try to balance it on one finger, where you decide to place your finger will determine the ability of the stick to stay balanced. If you place your finger too far towards one end, the stick will either waver violently or it will fall altogether. If you want the stick to balance, you must aim to put your finger as close to the centre point as possible.

The same is true with this!

Are there any quick fixes?

Let us just say that some 'fixes' are quicker than others. Recognising why you are carrying out a particular action can put you much closer to being able to control the action. If you can see that you are placing your finger too close to one end of the stick, you can move it along nearer to the centre, but that only works if you understand about balance – and even know that the stick has two ends!

Very often, people travel through life without really observing what is going on and certainly not making any attempt to understand it. It is very often easier not to. They may be used to living with a wavering stick! Or even one shaking violently, before it falls into an abyss! You must be awake to possibilities and to the fact that things can change.

To exercise free will, you need to know firstly that free will exists; you then need to decide to exercise it and start to be aware of what other opportunities exist. Having done that (and this is the difficult bit), you need to decide what you actually want and what will make you happy.

On earth, as it is in heaven, people often have absolutely no idea!

But getting back to your pain, as that is preoccupying your thoughts for today. Fortunately for you, your pain is muscular and will go in a few days. It is telling you to think more about your posture and to move more in a graceful way. It is telling you not to sit for long periods of time, especially not in an unbalanced posture! It is also telling you to think about what you really want in life, so that you start to create more of what you want and less of what you don't.

Here ends today's lesson.

CHAPTER 7
GETTING BOOKED IN

TUESDAY 5 DECEMBER 2017

Hello, Battrick.

Hello, Julie!

Thank you for turning up.

We have an arrangement.

Yes, we do, but not everyone always does what they say they are going to do, so 'thank you!'

What are we going to talk about today?

Death.

But what aspect of it?

The process: we are going to talk about what happens when you pass.

Is it the same for everyone?

No, but there are similarities and things that must take place.

Do we have any sort of choice about how and when we pass?

Absolutely!

Well why (on earth) would people choose to go so young, and in distressing ways?

They have their reasons, as we have discussed before, but today I want to talk about the process.

OK

We book you in. That is the first thing to notice.

Everyone has a specific time, otherwise there would be chaos.

What about when there is some disaster and lots of people go at once?

If it is booked in, it really doesn't matter. One, one hundred, one

thousand, one million.

What does "booking in" consist of?

The people who are going to meet you need to be on stand-by. We try to avoid people coming back on their own and there are often many people this side who want to be present. They need to know what time to turn up!

We need to have what you might understand as 'decompression tanks' ready. There is no physical, so nothing physical needs to be done, but the soul needs to adjust and realise that it no longer has a body to restrict it and it needs to be awakened to the fact that it has returned to its source. Otherwise it could be wandering around thinking it is on earth or another physical realm, rather than back home. We want to avoid unnecessary shock after what can be a traumatic experience.

The soul at a deep level knows when a physical body is coming to an end but it will, in many cases, have been under the illusion that there is no afterlife. The acceptance of an afterlife might not have been beneficial to its subject's life. With reinforcement, the soul will start to believe what the mind and physical body have been telling it: when you die, that is it – no more, nothing else, return to dust. If the death is sudden then there is no time for the soul to adjust. That is why what I am terming a decompression tank is needed. The amount of time that a soul spends in there is related to their views and expectations. Someone who had a deep acceptance and understanding of the afterlife, such as yourself, might only need to be in there for a few brief moments in time. For others it could be some considerable time, but there is no reason to put earthly timescales on this as they are completely meaningless in our terms.

What happens in these tanks?

Mainly rest. The soul rests, with interested parties 'sitting' with them and waiting for them to realise where they are.

Are these interested parties family members who have previously passed?

In many cases yes, but some will be from past lives and there are also souls around who dedicate their heavenly lives to doing this work. Some of these souls have never had an earthly life and appreciate the help of family or others to help guide the waking soul.

What else happens in the tank – what does it look like?
I know this is difficult for you to understand, but where there is no physical realm, what something looks like it just an illusion and can vary from person to person. Many people see it as a bed. So when their soul starts to awake, they 'see' themselves lying on a bed surrounded by familiar faces.

During the time they are there, they are shown (or replayed) events from their lives. Some of these will be happy memories and others may be memories they would rather forget. The objective is to enable souls to make an assessment of their lives and progress by understanding what they have learnt on the journey through life.

Some of these learning messages are very minor and others can be traumatic: a realisation that they acted in a way which was not beneficial to the souls around them. Or it can be positive reinforcement that they achieved what they set out to do.

The point is, they (the souls) judge themselves. No one tells them, there is no punishment to make them feel better or anything that might justify their actions in their thoughts, this is self-judgement pure and simple.

How do people react to this?
Many people who have committed crimes in one life may have been looking for some sort of absolution in the next. They may expect that they will be forgiven by an entity other than themselves. But this would not require any effort on their part and would lack the responsibility necessary to move to the next stage. They have to forgive themselves, but this has to be meaningful and not empty words – which have no

meaning on our side of the fence anyway, but that is another discussion!

In order to forgive yourself, you first have to acknowledge what you have done. You have to accept that you had free will and you exercised it in a particular way. Situations can be very complex, of course, and some souls feel they were coerced into committing crimes, and then there are issues of power and response, but eventually people have to accept that on some level there was some exercise of their own free will and that had a particular response. They then have to believe that they had a choice and could have made other, more beneficial decisions. After that, they need to acknowledge that the decisions they made were not the best and caused harm or distress to others (on whatever level the soul may be dealing with). After that, they need to forgive themselves and decide what they would do differently if they were put (or put themselves) into that situation again.

At the end of it they are 'decompressed' and released back into the afterlife with a greater level of understanding than if they had just walked back as they were.

Family (and this is soul group family, physical life family and empathic souls) come to help the newly-entered soul back into what they will realise is their normal existence.

I used the word 'decompression' as it is bringing the soul back to the frequency required to conduct its work on this plane.

Phew, so do they go there immediately – what happens first to book them in?

As you have suspected, the decision to return home can be delayed or even brought forward should a soul require it. If a physical life is pressing too heavily on a delicate soul, then some decide to hasten their return to get back sooner. Others are having a much better time than they thought and decide to stay on longer! This can be as a result of choices they made during their lives, or it could be because they want to be around for a specific earthly or physical event. The birth of a child, to see someone get married, or get married themselves, to visit somewhere, or just to spend more time with the ones they love.

You have often seen people who seem to decide that they are not ready to go and make a decision to stay around longer.

Yes, I know this is true of my own mother. She wanted to prepare me for her death and was trying to stay as long as possible to support me, so I would be ready. When it came near the time, she was determined that she wouldn't pass on her grandson's birthday. She thought that would have been awful. As it was, she went the day before. I know that with my father, who was ill and at death's door a couple of years before, he really wanted to experience the millennium. It was something that he had heard about as a young child and he always hoped he would be around to experience it. We had a great party – I danced with him and he was dead a few months later.

Good, so you understand there is free will when it comes to death, too. However, the physical body has its limitations and sometimes the soul's vessel can let you down before you expect it. In that case, you may find that it cannot be repaired and you may decide that the associated pain and trauma is far worse than you thought and for this reason the only viable option is to return to source. Sometimes these people can decide to reincarnate/be reborn relatively quickly and start again.

For as many souls as there are, there are as many situations that require handling. The decompression tank therefore provides an important service.

So, whenever the approximate time has been determined by the soul – either as they preordained prior to incarnation, or as a result of decisions made since – there has to be a more accurate time, in the same way you might need to book a bed in a hospital.

I think I know what you are going to say. When I was sitting with my

own mother and watching her die, around 30 hours before she did pass,
I 'saw' a 'monk', as I will describe him (although no face was visible
and he appeared to be in grey/white) doing what looked like taking my
mother's pulse and making some sort of judgement about how long she
had left. I had never believed in the Grim Reaper and I thought this
was just something from horror stories and Hallowe'en costumes, but
I started to see how this legend had come about. Although I am not
sure if this takes place in the case of a sudden death on the road, for
example.

In order to answer this, we have to discuss the synchronicity of events.
If someone is 96 and lying on their death-bed, determined that they do
not want to die on their grandson's birthday, having done everything
they wanted to do in life and being ready to go, then the synchronicity
of them passing at a particular hour is very high.

If someone is healthy and decides to take a particular journey on a
busy motorway at a moment's notice, and another car has someone in
it who at that moment decides to look away from the road ahead and
check a message on their phone, then the synchronicity of that situation
resulting in death is much lower. A series of events must come into play at
exactly the right (or, for the subjects involved, the 'wrong' time) in order
for death to take place. The speed at which the emergency crew arrive
at the scene (did the paramedic need the toilet before they left, and was
that the result of an extra cup of tea at breakfast?); was it raining and
was traffic slower, increasing the time for the emergency crew getting
there? How busy was the hospital? Was the optimum number of staff
available to treat the patient? Was the best neurosurgeon on leave that
day, because her daughter was in a concert that afternoon and she didn't
want to miss it? What if the person who sent the text message had just
waited a second or two longer?

With a different set of circumstances, or even one circumstance playing out rather differently, the death might not have occurred. We can work out the probability of the synchronicity based on other circumstances as well and have an idea whether death is likely to take place that day (or even a few days later, or a month/a year later).

Do events in the cosmos have an impact, too? I am just thinking about horoscopes, etc. and whether astrological events have an impact.

I am sure you will not be surprised to hear me say that your horoscopes are an over-simplification of cosmic events that may or may not impact.

There are cosmic events that have an impact on earthly events, such as earthquakes and tidal heights, and these can result in deaths. The position that the planets are in when someone is born has an impact on their personality and the likelihood of events taking place during their lifetimes, but souls decide to incarnate at specific points so that they can contribute to life at certain phases. The individual movement of planets within a lifetime may have less impact than some people currently believe, although they can contribute to the synchronicity of events taking place.

(My telephone rang and I took a call.)

I am getting the impression that this is it for today.

Yes – the telephone ringing was an example of a synchronistic event that had an impact on our communication. However, keep in mind that the passage of time for us is different and one synchronistic event on its own does not dramatically change the course. There needs to be a sequence of synchronistic events in this case to have an impact on the outcome.

CHAPTER 8
THE JOURNEY

I was a few minutes late arriving at my computer and as I write this it is 8.03 am. I am not sure that Battrick is here.

He seems to be telling me from a distance that he can't be here and we are going to do twice a week from now on. It is a bit like someone calling on the phone to say that they won't make a meeting,

At any rate, I don't think there is anything doing today.

(Next day)

THURSDAY 7 DECEMBER 2017

Battrick is here today. For some reason I am still having difficulty with his name! I keep wanting to call him Battik.

The other day, Battrick, we were talking about the decompression-type tank that souls arrive in when they first pass. I can sort of see the connection, but can you describe these, please, and is there another name we can use?

Ah, names ... very important!

I can see the joke .... nice that you have a good sense of humour when working with me!

Names are important, which is why I correct you each time you get mine wrong!

If you don't like 'decompression tank' then let us see what you would prefer to call it.

I can see that you are making the connection with people who come up too quickly from scuba-diving and risk getting the bends. I know that they are

fed pure oxygen to equalise their blood levels, or something like that.

When someone passes they need to equalise to the frequency here, but more than that, it gives their soul time to adjust.

What would you prefer to call it?

I have absolutely no idea, but if 'decompression tank' is the best name then that it shall of course remain as that.

I hesitate in asking this question, but do lots of people go in, or are they individual?

The point is that to the person/soul concerned it appears to be an individual experience, with family and friends close by. That is all that matters. We can create an illusion of anything in order to ease the transition. The 'mechanics', if you will, of what is actually happening are of little consequence to you. The point is that as far as the soul is concerned, they are in there on their own.

Can we get back to the Grim Reaper, please? You mentioned about the probability of someone passing at a particular time and how you could anticipate even sudden death, but what role does the Grim Reaper play?

Well, the first thing to note is that there is more than one! It is rather an unfortunate name for a rather kindly group of monks who carry out this role.

And what do they do?

You might describe it as 'admin'. They look at the probability and then visit the person to assess the most appropriate time to pass. In the case of your mother this would have been a simple operation, as they would assess the physical body and establish a time when that physical body would no longer support the soul. They then inform relatives and friends of the time of passing, in case they wish to be present. I hesitate to use this comparison, because things do not work like this over here, but they 'enter the person into our computer system to show that a return is imminent'.

This is putting the process into words you can understand, because all our systems are organic.

Organic?

Yes, what you might understand as mind-generated, rather than machine-generated, but the end result is the same. There is a record that someone will return at a particular point in time.

What happens in the case of sudden death? Can that probability change right up to the last minute?

It can and does, and of course death can become more likely as well as less likely during the course of one of your earth days. This is based on all the reasons we discussed earlier.

I am getting the impression you are a bit uncomfortable discussing this.

In some ways I am. The death process is a very personal thing and different for all concerned. The reasons for death are multitudinous and come about because of decisions taken before and during life. It is far too trite to dismiss these reasons in a few sentences and try to describe a generic process. That is why I am uncomfortable. However, I appreciate the need to find the right words to explain this situation to you.

The fact is, earthly words do not exist to describe what happens and therefore I must find the most appropriate words resident in your database, or something you might be able to relate to later. Hence using the expression 'decompression tank'.

This is just a quick question here regarding cryogenics – is there any way on this planet that people can come back to life after being frozen?

What do you think? When the soul leaves the body at some point after death then it returns to the afterlife. If the physical body is frozen then it can be kept in a state of suspended animation, but why would anyone want to do that if the soul has already left? Why, having returned home, would a soul wish to re-inhabit a body that it gave up because it was either old or riddled with disease, and had already died?

But is it technically possible?

A soul can inhabit bodies that are not their own – this does happen, but with so much choice, I cannot understand why it would want to inhabit something that was not fit for purpose in the first place.

Familiarity?

Possibly, yes, but extremely unlikely. What I can tell you is that it has not happened yet!

Is there anything more you can tell me about the Grim Reaper?

What do you want to know?

What do you call them?

Ah, names again!

I know you saw one when you mother died, what was your impression?
I saw a hooded figure that to me was either white or very light grey. I got the impression the person was male and had the demeanour of a doctor or a nurse – I am wondering now why I thought them male! I could only see the hood and arms. They certainly did not appear to be like pictures I have seen in horror films. There was no skeleton visible. Just a hooded and efficient person comes to mind.

They are extremely efficient, as they have to be. They are what you might describe as monks, although most have not had an earthly life. They are seen by some people and this is where the story comes from.

I was amazed and it took me a while to realise what it was! I honestly had never believed in stories of the Grim Reaper.

Another unfortunate name.

So, what happens after the decompression tank?

Gradually souls emerge and take up life on this side.

What does 'take up life on this side' mean?

That is a tale for next week.

So, we have come to the end again? It is only 8.30 am – I could have gone on for another hour!

You maybe, but I can't.

Communication of this type is quite exhausting. I must align my frequency to yours.

Can I do anything to help this process?

Not really, you need to remain grounded in order to capture the earthly words. It is more difficult when I have to find the right words to present to you. You perceive this as seamless, but for me this is a much longer process. I have to extract the words from your 'database', then I have to articulate them to you on a frequency you can hear. This takes time and from my perception, there are very long time gaps that are imperceptible to you. The more I have to do that, the less time I can maintain the communication for.

I do appreciate what you are doing for me!

Many thanks.

TUESDAY 12 DECEMBER 2017

Hello, Battrick – are you there?

Yes.

Are we still able to work today?

Yes.

What aspect are we talking about today?

Battrick, what about your normal day? What am I keeping you from, or what else do you have to fit into your day?

The concept of 'day' is interesting, too, as compared to your awareness of what a day feels like. Some humans adopt 'days' in order to impose some familiarity on events over here, but it is not necessary. We don't have working days, or working weeks, or even weekends. We are just 'here' in every sense of the word. Here means living in the present. We are not wondering about the past or pondering on the future, because neither exists in the way you understand them.

We therefore just concern ourselves with our immediate present or 'presence'. We are present at all times. There is no sleep time, or unconscious wandering of the mind. There is no physical state, so such a concept is not necessary. Also, it is not needed in order to receive messages from otherworldly sources. We have everything we need here; we are just present in the moment.

What is it like living like that? I cannot imagine not wondering/ worrying about tomorrow. What will happen next, if something I said was misconstrued, etc.

I have been in this state so long that for me this is my normal state, so it is difficult to answer that question. Worrying/wondering about past or future has no meaning for me. I can travel through all the possibilities and make the best choice that is in line with my desires and impacts least on others.

I spend far too much of my life worrying about what might be, or what I should have done. I spend more time thinking than doing and that means that when something needs doing, I am normally rushing to catch up!

These are not concepts we entertain.

What does your day feel like?

As I communicate with people living in physical realms then I have to adopt the concept of time as you understand it. Otherwise I would not know when you were planning to meet with me! I plan these sessions into my present state.

Not your future state?

No, because everything that ever was or can be is laid out in front of me.

I just follow one of the paths to get to where I am expecting to be.

This is complicated to get my head round.

Understandably.

Living fully in the present is not possible in your physical realm. You must abide by the constructs of time as you understand them. Planets spin and there is night and day. The body needs rest to function and the mind needs a lack of stimuli to process everything that has happened.

Is this why I sometimes wake up in the morning with a solution to something? A problem I maybe did not even know existed when I went to sleep?

That question needs to be answered twofold. Your brain needs to order stimuli for the preservation of its health. It is no coincidence that people who are sleep-deprived become ill very quickly, both physically and mentally. The other part of the answer involves your soul's connection with its spiritual source. Loved ones and guides use your sleep time to get messages to you. Not all the time, of course, but when they think you need to be aware of something. They/we are in the position to see all those possibilities, which you cannot. Someone who loved you in your physical life will not stop loving you in the afterlife. They will not/cannot interfere with your free will, but what they can do is to show you alternatives and options during your sleep time. Many try to do this during your waking time, too!

The ability of a subject to 'hear' advice from the spirit world varies from person to person. Some hear easily, others hear but do not want to believe, and others can be shouted at from our side and still appear not to notice. 'Fate' has a habit of stepping in and the signs can become more obvious, but – and let us be absolutely clear about this – these are only suggestions and everyone has free will. Their free will overrides anything else.

So, to see if I have this right, if someone is following a particularly destructive path, a loved one from the spirit world might attempt to contact them in their sleep and show them alternative life-styles, or how a problem might be overcome.

Yes, they may not remember once awake, but the 'message'/thought intention is still there. It has started to take on its own life. The subject may see something during the day that reinforces their dream image (of which they may be totally unaware and say they never remember dreams); the seed has been set, but if the subject wishes to pursue the lifestyle that their loved ones believe is detrimental to the subject's happiness then there is little that can be done. Free will will always override intention imposed by others. This is true whether the so-called helpful soul is on the physical or the spiritual plane.

So, getting back to your question, what does my day feel like? Probably very different to yours!

Eating is not required, but many people recreate the sensation of eating and the community of it. Eating is something that is so ingrained in physical life that it can be a while before people passing abandon it.

I do enjoy eating and going out for meals with friends, but it is so time-consuming and takes up so much of our day preparing and eating meals. I can see how you could save time by not doing this!

You could save time, if time existed – which it doesn't. Not in the way you are using the word, anyway.

Imagine sitting in a large organic sphere. Everything that ever was or ever could be or would be is accessible from the centre. Whatever you do, you are returned to the centre, although the centre is not always in the same place.

It moves?

No, your soul's perception of it moves, but that is all.

Within this sphere you can interact with others outside the sphere – either in their own sphere, which has the ability to meld with yours, or beyond the spheres in different dimensions. Within the sphere, you can create whatever you feel necessary and desire just by thinking about it.

However, with creation comes responsibility.

But if nothing is real and can be changed – where does the responsibility bit come in?

There is responsibility to yourself and to others to create things that are beneficial to all. There are no rules, other than those we impose on ourselves. By seeing the outcome of everything immediately, we are able to make choices that impact positively on ourselves and others.

Can I have an example, please?

A farmer decides to buy a tractor to harvest corn from a field. The tractor saves the work of many people and the corn is harvested more quickly. However, as everyone is doing the same thing at the same time, the price of the corn becomes very cheap for a few weeks a year. There is too much to be stored and processed, and it starts to go bad. The people who used to cut the corn by hand no longer have a job. They cannot feed their families and their children starve. The farmer cannot pay his monthly bill for the tractor, as the price of corn has fallen so low. He finds that his farm has become uneconomical to run and closes it. The price of corn rises again, as he is not the first person to do this, and poor people remain hungry, as they have no job and no chance of buying the higher-priced corn to feed their families.

So, he shouldn't have bought the tractor in the first place?

If he/she had seen some of the possible outcomes before he bought a tractor then he might have picked something else.

He could have rented a tractor, or continued to collect the corn by hand?

Yes, renting one would have reduced the costs, he would still have needed some of his workers for other jobs throughout the year. He might have had the idea to diversify some of his crop production and even grow vegetables. But to do this, he would need to consider alternatives. In his

ANSWERS FROM THE OTHER SIDE

limited world, where everyone only grows corn, it could be a long time before he thinks of other things he could do. This is where dreams come in – either his own mind creates alternative scenarios or loved ones from another realm provide a few ideas during sleep. The farmer can choose to ignore all other options and continue the original path, or he may wake up with what he might call the 'inspiration' to do something else. This action might be reinforced by a chance meeting, or hearing a stranger talking. His mind will now be more receptive to ideas which reinforce his intention. These are the seedlings of creation.

I can see that this level of insight would be very valuable here. Why can we not see the bigger picture, as you can?

It is to do with the density of the energy on your planet.

Explain.

You are operating at a lower frequency and you can only be aware of all the 'present options' when you start to operate at a higher frequency.

How do we do this?

You cannot do it completely on a physical plane, but with meditation and listening to your feelings and heart you can start to operate in this way more effectively.

You can play out scenarios in your mind. This is open to everyone, but very few people choose to do it. They see what they want to see as the outcome – good or bad!

Julie, you should know that there are no 'Brownie points', as you call them, in the afterlife, just as there is no punishment. We take responsibility for every choice we make and everything we create (what you might describe as good or bad). If you do things because you are looking for praise from a source outside yourself then I must make it clear that it does not work like that.

Equal opportunities mean that no one can bestow or remove praise. In fact, as a concept it does not exist. We judge ourselves, although the word 'judge' implies a punishment pending and that is not true, either. By being at one in the present and seeing everything that ever was or could be, we live in harmony with each other and the various universes that we support.

Much of our existence is concerned with helping souls residing on physical planets. Souls take many forms, but the density of the existence means they need guidance – although they can decide whether to take it.

Is life boring – knowing what is going to happen all the time?

Some souls elect to undertake a physical existence to understand life on earth, etc. It is true to say that not knowing all the possibilities can be an exciting proposition for a time. It is also a test for the soul, to see if they can make decisions when away from the source that is in line with their source's intentions.

Others elect to help people on earth more directly from the spirit world, as I am doing with you and others.

Are you happy?

In the context that you understand it, then I can say 'yes'.

And in your context?

If I experience happiness, then it must be possible to experience pain and sadness, and from this dimension those emotions do not exist. Living in this way means that things just 'are' and they are devoid of emotions that I might place on them, as this is an unnecessary way to exist and not relevant to my soul's existence.

It is all sounding a bit 'cold'.

I did warn you that it was not all love, light and fluffiness!

But what is the purpose of it all, Battrick?

Does existence always need a purpose? Do we always have to be travelling in what you perceive to be a forward direction? Can we not just 'be'?

To be honest Battrick, on earth, I am not sure we can!

(I am getting the idea that this is the end of our communication today).

CHAPTER 9
FUNERALS

Battrick – are you here today?

Yes, I am here

What are we going to talk about?

Funerals

Oh, OK, what about them?

When someone dies, there needs to be a transition period from this world to the next. I have already told you about the 'decompression tank', although you did not like this phrase, but there is a process that needs to be completed from your side, too.

The soul is connected to the physical body by 'gossamer strands' even after the soul has left it. There is an energetic connection that must be cut for the soul to be completely free. There are many ways that this can be done, but a funeral is a good place to start.

Not everyone has a funeral, of course, and not all bodies are recovered.

How critical is this process? Will souls suffer if there is no funeral?

Let us be clear: the physical body does not have to be physically present when this process happens. It provides a convenient disposal mechanism for the soul, and for family and friends who have loved the physical appearance of the person who has died. Everyone who had been close (emotionally and physically) may have a strand connection to the body that needs to be removed.

Well, what happens if it isn't?

People might remain more emotionally and physically connected to the remains. Even in ash form, this is not a particularly desirable thing to happen. There is much to be said about grieving, and this will be dealt with in a later section, but some people decide to keep the ashes of their partner or parent/much-loved friend, as they still want to feel close to them and may just not be ready to part with what remains of them at that time. Or they may just be waiting to get other family members together to scatter the ashes. This can happen after the strands have been cut and provide a further level in the grieving process, and can be beneficial to people. There is no issue with that, but if someone wanted to interact with the remains then the soul would not be completely free.

Interact?

It is not unheard of for people who cannot mentally accept the death of a loved one to secrete remains in a place that only they know of and even talk to the decomposing body, believing that the soul is still present. This is not desirable for the soul that has passed or the person(s) mourning it. There are health considerations on the physical side, and unless the soul is free, they cannot fully adjust to life on this side.

This is starting to get rather macabre and I am thinking about how this conversation might be upsetting people who have just lost someone.

The majority of people go through some sort of process that marks the end of life. This is beneficial to the departed soul and to the people who remain on the physical side. There are certain things that need to be achieved for there to be a smooth transition for the soul, and knowing that their physical body has been dealt with is one of those things.

The actual terms of the event are immaterial. The important thing is that the soul is satisfied that their business on earth is complete, and that family and friends can start the grieving process. What words are said and what songs are sung are of no consequence to the process. However, souls often express gratitude at the thought their loved ones bestow on the event.

Can souls be present at their own funeral?

Yes, indeed they can, and at the funeral of others, or at other family/social events.

What about burial or cremation?

Again, the departed soul's preference should be respected, but from a process point of view it makes no difference at all.

It also, which may surprise you, does not make very much difference who is physically present at the event, or even if there is an event at all.

I thought you said that the strands needed to be cut and a funeral was a good place to start.

I did, and yes it is, but it is not the only way.

At the point of death, the soul starts to make its exit from the body. This can take a few seconds, a few minutes or a longer period, depending on the circumstances of death.

Having left – and the soul will take the fastest, easiest route out – it needs to assess its situation.

In the case of a sudden death, the soul may be surprised to see its physical body from outside of itself. It may wish to hang around to be absolutely sure that death has happened and this is not a temporary state.

Sometimes it is?

Yes, near-death experiences are well documented, as you know, and souls who find themselves outside of their body because of a sudden death, a death on an operating table, or in other places, may find that they re-enter their body a few minutes later and resume life; often reporting strange phenomena that frequently have the effect of changing their earthly lives. A subject might be told 'this is not your time' and they return to their bodies.

To resume, a soul will find itself outside of its body and, in the case of an unexpected death (to the soul/person anyway), they could decide to stay close to the body in order to protect it. For example, you take care of your body when your soul resides there: why would you suddenly leave it if you were unsure about what was happening?

So, the soul could and often does stay in the vicinity of the body for a period after death. It is important to note that this does not happen in all cases. Someone who is prepared for death, or who has been in pain, or is otherwise unhappy with their physical state, may leave and not ever look back. It is their free will and personal choice. That can be exercised during the death transition, as well as before and afterwards.

Funerals provide a stage of movement for all concerned.

By the time the funeral has been arranged (and this can vary a great deal in earth terms from country to country), the soul takes comfort in the fact that his or her physical body is being put to rest in one form or another.

As I said, the method of disposal is of no consequence if it is carried out in a way that feels comfortable and normal to the departed soul and their family. Words of various sorts have an energy of their own and can provide healing for both the people who remain and the departed soul.

Souls do not need to enter the decompression tank immediately. When they do, communication with the people left behind becomes more distant. Where there is uncertainty about the people left behind, or about the method of death, souls elect to stay earth-bound for a longer period of time. The important thing to note is that they have a choice.

A mother leaving young children might feel particularly bound to stay close to them until she is sure that they are able to manage without her. This is not always the case: someone who had an illness might have felt they had made good provision for their children and by the time the soul leaves their body they are at peace.

There is no one way, or one right way.

So, what exactly does the funeral achieve?

Besides the obvious one of providing a method of the physical disposal of physical remains, it gives families a chance to say things that they did not say while the person was alive. A soul does not need to hear words because they understand the emotion.

This can work both ways? Might the soul hear something they do not particularly like? Is this why people say never speak ill of the dead?

Yes, but maybe the comments will be useful in their soul's further development. They can see how much people cared, or might realise that they did not express sufficient emotion themselves and did not tell other people how they felt. They may realise of course that they were not particularly well liked, or were completely misunderstood.

Gosh, this is going to make some people think a bit! To know that departed souls can hear you talking about them after they have died!

I did warn you that there could be some shocking revelations and not everyone would want to hear what you have to say!

Personally, I think it is better to know! If you would not have said something to someone when they were alive then I think maybe we should not say something after they have gone.

Let us be clear, a soul can feel the emotion and the understanding. Words that might be said in grief or anger would be understood. People need not to be concerned about a few words spoken when they are having to come to terms with a passing. There was a lifetime to build up a relationship and people make mistakes on both sides of life. In the afterlife there is greater understanding, but whenever and wherever there is free will then souls do not always follow a smooth path.

So to recap, the funeral provides a method of disposal, a chance for the soul to see what everyone really thought about them and, for people living, a chance to say goodbye?

Yes, it is an opportunity, but for many it is just the start of the grieving process. Some people, after the death of a loved one, are never the same again and go about their business in an almost zombie state until their time has come. Sometimes there is no acceptance of the parting.

For many, eventually they manage to get on with their lives and if it was a close physical union, life will have changed but it will not be totally without value or joy. There is free will and choice about how people react to death. They can decide to wait for death themselves and hope it comes quickly, or they can embrace life and try to find a new life despite their sadness. Sometimes people need help from both planes to help them decide how they should react.

So what else does a funeral do? What about these strands?
A funeral as an event has an energy. It is the subject of the focus of attention and therefore the energy builds. When the event comes to an end, there is an acceptance by most that this particular life has come to an end, that any strands of emotion/love/feeling will not be reciprocated as they were before and the ties must be cut.

Although someone does not attend a funeral and think of it in these terms, they know that they will not be hearing from this person again and they need to adjust their thinking about them. They will not be at the pub, or the school, or the factory, or in their house. Therefore, subconsciously, the threads that held them together are severed and the soul will feel lighter at this point.

What happens if not everyone at the funeral feels like this?
The soul will know that some people will have more difficulty coping with their death than others. Many decide to fully pass to the other side in the knowledge that they can help them from there. From the other side they have a greater view of the possibilities of life for the people they left behind. The soul can decide to sever those strands themselves.

Does the decompression tank sever them?
The decompression tank serves many purposes and releasing negative earthly ties is one of them. You must understand that family love and bonds transcend lives. Personality remains. All the transition process does is to make living in the next world easier.

Negative ties?

The soul must rise to a higher frequency to experience the sensation of the afterlife. It can only do that if it is vibrating at a higher frequency than on earth. Negative associations from the earth plane have the effect of lowering the frequency. No one removes them, the soul takes responsibility for past actions and severs the ties from within the tank.

So, what does this tank actually do?

It provides a half-way house in terms of frequency. The level of frequency that a soul arrives at varies from person to person. As I said before, some people will spend very little time in the tank and others need much longer (although the perception by both parties might be the same). If a soul was released into the afterlife while still vibrating at a low frequency, they would not 'see', 'hear', 'feel' everything around them. If they did not raise their frequency, they would only be aware of things on a physical plane.

When someone from the spirit world makes contact, do they need to lower their frequency?

Yes, and the medium has to raise theirs, so that they meet in the middle.

Some spiritual souls are better at lowering than others. Some physical souls are better at raising theirs than others. This meeting in the middle is why we call them 'mediums'! Ha ha.

This is such an important point that I want to make sure I understand. At the point of death, or sometime shortly after death, your soul leaves your body. Depending on the circumstances of the death, the soul may stay with the body to make sure it has definitely left for good. In some circumstances a soul may return if, for whatever reason, it is not their time to go. In any circumstance, the soul can and often does stay around friends and loved ones to see how they react, and in doing so can hear what people are saying about them!

A funeral (whatever form that may take) provides a useful mechanism for disposing of the remains to the satisfaction of the departed soul and provides an opportunity for people to sever gossamer strands that connect them with the departed soul. It is also a chance for souls to feel appreciated and loved and they appreciate the efforts that people go to. I am assuming that souls attend their own funerals? They can certainly stay vibrating at a lower frequency for a while, but at some point they will need to enter what we are calling a decompression tank in order to raise their frequency to that of the afterlife.

In this tank, negative associations are removed by the soul (after some soul-searching?) in order to raise their frequency sufficiently.

To communicate with the earth plane, souls/people from either side need to meet in the middle.

This is of course an oversimplification, but it will suffice for now.

Thank you for your time and for coming down to my frequency.

We will leave it there for today.

CHAPTER 10
TO INTERTWINE

TUESDAY 19 DECEMBER 2017

It would have been my Mum and Dad's wedding anniversary today.

It still is!

Hello, Battrick!

Regardless of where they are in your perception, they were married on this day many years ago in your time.

Will they be celebrating?

Do they still live together?

They join together, but then they join with other souls as well. They may realise the significance of the date today for you and both join you.

What does this 'join' together mean?

In the absence of a physical existence, there is the opportunity to do more. There are no household chores, or food to buy and cook (unless a soul wishes to recreate these activities for comfort). Souls are free to roam and intertwine with whomsoever they wish!

'Intertwine?'

When there is no physical, there is no physical boundary. You might prefer to think of it as a 'meeting of minds'.

What happens if you don't fancy being 'intertwined'?

Then you don't do it! Equal opportunities and free will!

What are the advantages?

Communication, belonging (family/soul group), entertainment.

Entertainment?

Yes, why when you have free will would you NOT choose to be entertained

and to entertain?

There are so many concepts that need rethinking! I suppose somewhere in the back of my mind I am still thinking about sitting on a fluffy cloud and feeling serene!

If you wanted to create a feeling of sitting on a fluffy cloud and feeling serene then that is an opportunity open to you, but after a while you might wonder why you were doing it.

People who report back via mediums normally seem fairly happy.

When you talk to a friend on the phone who has not heard from you for a long time, you are anxious to tell them things, and that (in this case) you have been following their progress and you know about their lives. It is a rare opportunity and you are lucky to get the chance. This makes people on our side happy to pass on good news!

I suppose that is what it is: passing on good news!

Yes, isn't that what you are trying to do, too?

Yes, absolutely, but I just have concerns that some people will not interpret everything we are telling them as good news! If you have lost someone you didn't like, who was a bully in life and intimidated you, for example, to hear that they are following your every move from the spirit world would surely be a devastating thing to have to take on board!

They must accept some responsibility for picking up the book or downloading the file in the first place. They must have wanted to know – if only through curiosity. You cannot lie to protect people. The reality will surface in the end.

Yes. I am sure this is true. Or they could just decide that the book was written by a deluded woman bordering on insanity!

Yes, that will happen too. But if people want to peep through the letter-box of the door between them and the next world, if they – and you - put their hand inside and lift the flap to see what is beyond, then you must all take responsibility for what you see! You cannot unsee it! You wanted to know, there was a way you could see a limited tranche of life on the other side of the door and you decided to take it. It is not just your responsibility; it is theirs as well.

OK, so back to this 'intertwining'.

I repeat, there is no physical!

So physical, intimate liaisons are not desirable in the same way. There is no physical gratification of a physical liaison, so this aspect is not a driving force. That is not to say that you may not wish to recreate the intimacy experienced on earth, but in reality there is a meeting of minds that is much more rewarding in every 'sense'.

OK, sounds like there is some explaining to do here.

For a moment I am going to use the words Mind and Soul as being the same thing. The mind is a product of many lifetimes. Mind (soul) groups which feel comfortable with one another often choose to stay together. There is a familiarity and love in these sorts of liaisons. There are shared experiences through many lifetimes, in most cases, although the roles played vary.

Does this mean that your father in one life could be your mother in another, and vice versa?

And any combination you can think of!

So, when we are talking about physical relationships and recreating the physical intimacy, most minds would not think this type of creation either desirable or helpful. It is true that couples often choose to recreate lives on earth which mirror previous lives, and to some extent move along together in the afterlife, but after a while they choose to join a more fulfilling, larger group. They 'intertwine'.

OK, still not there with my understanding. Do they lose their individuality at this point?

To some extent, but they also gain understanding and synergy.

Synergy? Do I have this word correct? The sum of the whole is greater than the parts?

Exactly. You can join a group and later unjoin, but by then, just by being part of the mind group, your understanding is enhanced and 'the individual' is enhanced. Or, it has to be said, you dip your toe in the water to test a group and flit in and out until you are happy that this is for you.

Dip your toe? Is this like trying out a few caravan holidays before you decide to buy your own on the site?

I suppose you could say that. There are no requirements or 'should'. It is a meeting of mind souls. It will enhance the individual mind and the mind group, as intertwining of energy adds to the understanding of the group. But there is also free will, so any time an individual mind wants to leave then they can 'untwine'.

I have chosen this word deliberately. To twine and untwine implies that there is a solid and complex growth process that links a mind to the rest of the group. This is not a simple door opening as you came through at death: this is a process that requires some effort on both parts, yours and the group's. They need to be sure of what they are adding to their group energy and you need to decide if their energy is something you want to add to your energy.

So do some groups have an energy focus that is different to others?

Yes, there are specialisms, just as there are specialisms on earth. People are different and they have a wide variety of interests.

In life we have our family group and our work group, but we can have both. Is that possible there?

This sort of separation does not exist in the same way. Your soul group will probably contain many souls who were part of your physical existence on earth. Not all of them, but many/some of them.

Some souls choose to reincarnate in order to assist souls on earth.

They may have been from a mind group that specialised in helping souls who have difficulty operating in earth's atmosphere. When their work is done, they can return home and they will no doubt return to their original mind group, rather than the family soul group of the person they were attempting to help.

So, in my understanding, then:

Death cannot be avoided and when we go depends on a number of factors such as what we had originally decided and what we might have decided on earth as a result of us using our own free will.

At some point, we get 'booked in' by a monk and a time of death is established.

At the point of death, we can be/are met by people who care about us, but to a large extent we experience what we think we will, based on our religious and cultural beliefs. Or we might not even experience anything, if that was our expectation.

Correct.

We then go into what we are calling a decompression tank in order to prepare us for the afterlife. The amount of time that we spend in there varies from person to person and is dependent on need. At some point, we come out and may then choose to recreate conditions on earth, such as getting somewhere to live and meeting up with friends and family. Having done that for an undisclosed while we then join another group, as it will be more fulfilling.

That provides a good summary of what I have told you. It is making something that is vast and uncompromising simple and accessible.

Uncompromising? According to the Cambridge Advanced Learner's Dictionary, 'if people or their beliefs are uncompromising, they are fixed and do not change, especially when faced with opposition'. It can be 'harsh'. According to the Collins Dictionary, 'if you describe someone as uncompromising, you mean that they are determined not to change their opinions or aims in any way'.

Yes. Would you expect the universe to bend to you or you to bend to the universe?

Equal opportunities?

All energy exists. Separation is an illusion. Energy can change form, but it is still energy and eventually it returns to source. That source is uncompromising. It is what it is.

There is so much to take in!

So, we really are all one?

Yes, our essence is our source. By the meaning of the word 'source' (do you wish to look this up?) ...

'Source' (and I am paraphrasing here) means 'where it begins'; 'where you get it from', according to Collins Dictionary. According to the Oxford English Dictionary, 'a place, person, or thing from which something originates or can be obtained'.

How can you change your source, once creation has taken place? If you originate from one source, how can it be anything other than uncompromising?

I think I am getting the idea.

I suppose I am just anxious to portray life on your side as a 'better place' than here.

It is a very different place and many souls prefer it.

The communication today feels quite exhausting – why is that?

We are both searching for words to describe things that cannot normally be put into words. We are meeting each other half-way.

Once a soul has returned to their source, what happens next?

That is the subject of a much later communication. There is still plenty to tell you.

I suppose I am still looking for those fluffy clouds that make people feel all warm and cosy!

If so, maybe you should write a different book?

You wanted to know what people do all day. That was the request. You did not ask for platitudes that make people feel better about a natural process. You wanted to know what was beyond the door and that is what you are getting.

I am not really complaining! I just want to understand how everything works. You did warn me it would not be all fluffiness and love and light.

It is however a positive destination! We need to make this clear. It may not be everything people expect or hope, but it is a positive existence.

If you read about near-death experiences, people often report that they did not want to come back to earth.

If you think about how you feel when you return from a long journey and you walk into your home that has friends and family there whom you haven't seen for a very long time – it is like that. If you were happy in your home before you left, and most people are, then you might be sad the journey is over, but that feeling is replaced as soon as you see your loved ones.

That is it for today.

Note: the communication for this day was so exhausting that I didn't get round to checking, printing and double-saving the file until the following day. It felt like a very serious exchange and felt more laboured. The one the following day was lighter.

CHAPTER 11
CELEBRATIONS

Battrick – are you there?

Yes, I am here.

What are we going to do today?

We are going to talk about Christmas.

Do you have Christmas over there?

In a manner of speaking, yes!

Even people of other religions?

Religion is a faith and you do not need 'faith' that you will arrive at a destination when you are already there. This is true of every religion or belief system that you adopt on earth or any other planet in the universe.

So why do you celebrate Christmas, then?

I didn't say WE did. But we know that you do!

This applies to Hanukkah, Thanksgiving, Eid, Diwali and any other celebration/festival that was important when the person was alive. It is a time when families come together and if the celebration was important in the life that has just been relinquished then it can still be important afterwards. Rather than visit individuals, it is helpful if they are all in one place. Several departed souls come together, too. It is something enjoyed here. We are talking about Christmas today because you will be celebrating it in a few days.

So how does this all work, then?

At times that are special to different groups, we arrange to collect and be around to share the event with you. This requires some preparation from our side, too. We normally have advanced warning about what is planned and you talk about it for weeks beforehand. Not only that, we will have witnessed similar events in the past and know 'the pattern'. We are also aware of things that have changed during the year and that certain people will be in different places and that the pattern has changed. You might like to think of it as 'an invitation' to attend.

As with any communication, most souls cannot just float down from above on a whim and join in the fun. They need to set up their communication so that they can 'sense' and be aware of what is going on around them when their souls return to physical earth. They do not need to go through a decompression tank, as they would have done when they arrived, but some preparation is necessary so that they can adjust their frequency to that on the original host planet. You might like to think of it as tuning into a TV station.

What does that involve?

The process is similar to when a medium attempts to contact the spirit world. They need to lower their frequency through thought and intention. You might like to think of it as transcendental meditation. In other words, there has to be a willingness and intention to be aware, and with some practice, souls can then move around the group at a party very easily. If they 'hear' someone mention their earth name then they are more likely to sit in on that conversation, but otherwise they will enjoy the session like everyone else.

Do they all 'enjoy'?

Well, naturally some souls are rather dismayed at what happens after their death and they might decide to intervene to help family members over time.

How much intervening can they do?

Just mainly through dreams and messages – not all are heard! With some persistent effort they can sometimes encourage family members to 'see' something they would not normally have seen. But, as we have said many times, there is free will, so although a message is received, it does not mean it is acted upon.

You have mentioned that souls join their groups and 'intertwine'; how does this work in terms of visiting family and friends at Christmas?

A whole group can visit or individual souls 'untwine' and visit in smaller groups.

Not individually?

For the soul to have joined the soul group in the first place, there must have been some commonality and so it is quite likely that more than one soul would attend these events. It is the same when someone dies. Previously-departed souls come from what you would understand as different geological places to attend. In reality they are milliseconds apart, but I am trying to put this into words you, and everyone else, can understand.

It is helpful to know what the plans are! Transitioning souls from earth to 'heaven' are 'booked in' and festivals, weddings and births are known in advance. It just means that the necessary preparation takes place from our side, too.

Do departed souls have to attend?

No, absolutely not, and often they decide not to. The connection to the family now celebrating could be very slim. For example, a grandmother might know that her grand-daughter (now in her 90s) is celebrating her last Christmas on earth but she may not have any connection to the rest of the people attending. She knows that her grand-daughter will be joining her shortly and may choose not to attend. It is not compulsory!

So, what do they do when they attend these events?

Well, first let us talk a bit more about the communication process.

The living souls in the family being observed are, for the large part, not aware or not thinking about their departed souls. No attempt is being made to communicate at Christmas or any other time of the year.

Therefore, the communication is one way: from our side. Some souls find it much easier than others to switch between (I am going to use the words you are familiar with) earth and heaven.

This also means the view of the earth proceedings is experienced in a slightly different way, too. For many souls who have been in the spirit world for a while, this will be experienced in a similar way as you experience things on earth. They can sit beside someone and listen to a conversation. They can watch a favourite TV programme with you and see how you cook a meal. If there was an acceptance of an afterlife when the person was on earth then acceptance of an earthly life, at least initially, will assist in this process.

For newly-departed souls, and ones who perhaps have less interest in this communication, the experience could be like looking through a foggy window. There has to be an intention for the soul to 'want to see' what is going on. If they are impartial, or have little interest and decide just to drop by for a moment or two, then the view will not be so good. What I am saying is, that this type of communication requires preparation, practice and effort!

If there was a close family connection, or a departed soul senses a need from the earth side, then they are usually very willing to make the effort to see their loved ones.

Do they ever get upset about what they see? Family members on earth squabbling and being sad?

It depends what you mean by 'upset'. We have a broader view of events from here. We can see that motivations and words do not have to be spoken out loud for them to be understood.

So you are saying that departed souls visiting earth can read our minds, too?

If they wish to do so – there is no difference to us between a spoken word and one that remains unspoken. They are all thoughts and thoughts have energies that we can read. Whether you say something or not makes very little difference.

Oh dear! This will be a shock to some people.

Why should it be? A thought can be acted upon. It is better to monitor your thoughts to make sure they are positive and uplifting to people. If there is a big thought focus on doing someone harm, then the energy of that thought takes on life. Once created, it has the ability to turn on the person who created the original thought, and not just the person it was destined for. Thoughts resonate throughout your body. There is no separation, so if a thought is unkind (such as, I want to do that person harm), you are in fact creating an energy of harm that is resonating throughout your body and doing YOU harm.

You might understand it as: 'what goes around comes around'.

So in answer to your original question, 'what do they do when they attend these events?', it very much depends on what is going on and what they want to do. If the family event is quiet and one person is sitting in front of the TV watching a film and feeling very lonely because the departed soul is no longer on earth, then they might decide to just sit with them and tune into their thoughts to see if they can offer some words of comfort. This can be very powerful and can of course happen at any time – they do not have to wait until Christmas!

Offer 'words of comfort'?

They can attempt to imprint ideas, thoughts, solutions into the mind of the recipient. Whether they are received or not will depend on the state of mind of the person receiving the thoughts and even if received, whether they decide to act upon any suggestions.

These are only suggestions and ideas, in the same way that the person may have communicated suggestions when they were alive. Free will on both sides! It is important to remember this.

The recipient, of course, will not be aware that anything has taken place.

I can see why it is so important to monitor your thoughts!
In any situation where you feel someone is watching you, you either decide that it doesn't matter and get on with your life, forget all about it, or take the message and get on with your life.

In general, and this is an important message to get across about life, and not just death: a thought is almost the same as an action. Many negative thoughts lead eventually to a negative action. All negative thoughts have the ability to turn back on you, as they spend so long in your aura. Monitoring your thoughts to ensure they are positive and uplifting will enhance your life, but at the same time you do need to stay grounded and realistic about what is happening.

You cannot sit on your imaginary fluffy cloud and think that you do not have a place in your world. If there are problems that require you to think badly of a person, then it is better to put your energy into solving those problems.

We seem to have got off the Christmas topic!
Yes. We make preparations from our side to share important events with you, whatever they may be. Our communications and observations are not limited to these times, but more souls decide to 'join in' at more significant events from their perception, and Christmas is one of these.

You do not need to lay extra places at the table! Eating your food is not something we would be able to do! We do however like to join in the fun and see all the positive energy that can be created at these important times.

But it is not like that for so many families!
And in those cases, our community means that no one is alone, even though they think they may be.

Now that is a very positive thought!
Glad you think so.

CHAPTER 12
THE VALUE OF EVIDENCE

Before starting this communication, I woke up with the idea that I might be able to capture an orb of Battrick. Some people believe that these light forms on photographs are actual spirits. I am not sure what I think! The phenomenon only seems to work with digital cameras, as opposed to phones. I have one camera that I have used in the past to photograph orbs: it is a small Fujifilm Z35. I could not remember whether I used to use 'flash on' or 'flash off' mode, so I tried both and to be honest I cannot remember which yielded the best results. As far as possible, I have tried to look for other sources of light that might create this phenomenon: reflection from a street light outside my office window; reflection from some Christmas decorations that were still around, etc. I took some pictures before starting the 8am communication just randomly around the room. I captured a few 'orbs', but I am honestly not sure that they would convince anyone of anything, so I have decided not to include them.

Good morning, Battrick – Happy New Year!
I notice you have been trying to capture me on your camera.
Yes, is that OK?
It is not a problem.
I have captured a few orbs – thank you!
Did you doubt I was here?
No, honestly no, but it is nice to see some evidence – not just for me, either.

What are we going to talk about today? I suppose orbs of light would be an obvious choice?

No, that is not on the agenda now.

So, what is? Lights in general?

Evidence in general.

It is difficult to provide anything that anyone believes. That adage 'for those who believe, no proof is necessary and for those who don't, no proof is possible' is true, as far as I can tell. People do not WANT to believe a lot of the time and I know that by doing this they are going to think me a charlatan.

They will think that of us both!

Only if they accept your existence in the first place!

Human nature, being what it is, somehow needs 'proof'. Even believers need proof sometimes and that is why I was trying to capture something that would provide the believers with a little more evidence.

Even when you think that is impossible?

Yes, because I must try. Is there anything you can suggest?

This book is your 'evidence'. People reading this will know on one level or another that the words you speak (we speak) are true. Your words will resonate with them because you are not telling them something they don't know, you are reminding them of something they do.

Every soul on this planet has gone through the door between life and death many hundreds of times. Memory of the worlds in-between clears as they transcend into different worlds. It has to, otherwise they would be trying to get home and they need to live in the world they are in. It is the only way they can learn from it. Too much preoccupation with what went before or will come afterwards does not help them to settle.

Why do people come to earth, if life is better somewhere else?

It is not a matter of what is considered 'better', it is about experience and learning development. It is not possible to experience extremes in what you are calling heaven. The polarity does not exist in the same way, as souls are already in the centre and when in the centre of something, the extremes of experience exist beyond everyday existence.

I sort of think I know what you are saying, but an example would be good.

We talked about placing your finger on a stick and trying to balance that stick in mid-air. If your finger is in the exact middle, it is easy to balance it and stop it waving about. If it is off-centre then you must move your finger around a lot to keep the balance. If your finger is placed too far towards one end then keeping any balance at all is impossible and the stick will fall to the ground.

In heaven your finger (if we continue this analogy) is placed 'dead' centre (joke). On earth and many other planets that operate at different frequencies to ours, your finger is off-centre. If it is too far off then it is difficult to maintain any life at all, but some distance off and you can still move your finger to maintain some sort of balance. That is the way you can experience extremes and appreciate everything that experiencing extremes can teach you.

You appreciate love when you have seen hate; stability when you have experienced instability; and tiredness when you have experienced energy. But if the stick waves too much, in an uncomfortable position, then knowing that you can drop the stick and return to source is not as helpful as learning to move your finger to maintain the balance where you are.

One shows learning, the other shows defeat.

How important is all this learning? I thought if heaven was the ideal then why do people need to learn anything at all?

Souls have different, varying levels of growth. In order to grow, you need to be able to see where you could be if you did. If you can perceive no difference, why would you bother? Why would you put the effort in?

So, to recap, you are saying that in order to grow in heaven, you have to come to earth or another planet and experience extremes?

You need to learn how to balance extremes and how to appreciate the more desirable condition.

OK. And forgetting (mostly, anyway) where you have come from helps you to do this?

Yes, but when things are perceived very negatively on earth, or on whatever physical plane a soul finds itself, there is a need to remind them that a greater good exists. Note I say 'remind'. Not teach, not force them to see – just remind.

And not everyone wishes to remember?

Some souls integrate themselves into the life they are experiencing, to the extent that they do not believe anything else is possible. They take comfort in the fact that a long sleep awaits them at the end and everything is as it appears to the five senses they have brought with them. They no more believe in an afterlife than they do UFOs, in some cases.

And they are happy with that?

It depends on the personality type. Some are, and they find the earth plane easier to cope with if they deny any knowledge of a previous existence. Others believe that otherworldly things are possible, but their belief in their religion prevents them from accepting it.

I have come across this before. Anyone who is a medium or a psychic is accused of worshipping the devil!

But to accept an idea of a devil or of God implies that some sort of otherworldly life is possible.

But only to those people who are 'pure of soul', in my understanding. It doesn't matter what crimes they have committed on earth: as long as they accept Jesus in their final moments, the slate is clean! Sorry, Battrick, I have been to church on and off over the years, but I am not expert on religious scripture of any type. I find much of it contradicts what I know to be true and therefore, despite my best efforts, the lack of tolerance always gets to me and I put the book down or decide not to go back.

People have their own reasons and denounce whatever they wish to denounce, and some people will do this with your book.

What can I do about that?

Absolutely nothing, they have free will to think and express their opinion. They cope with their earthly life by following a teaching, and the predictability and the set of rules gives them a great deal of comfort. They live in the knowledge that something better awaits them and, depending on what religion it is, that all their earthly sins will be forgiven. A lot of this sentiment is true. Religion can support people as their earthly sticks flail around, and by denying communication with anything other than a God figure (and that privilege is only available to high priests and to bishops), they must make the best of their earthly lives.

But some people commit awful crimes in the name of religion – what about those?

They are exercising their free will, even if that free will involves giving away their personal power to people whom they respect and feel know better than they do. There are all sorts of other issues about making a difference and earning respect from peers.

But to give up your life and take young children with you through the most awful death … why/how?

I do not have all the answers you seek. Individuals exercise their own free will in the way they see fit. I am not able to look into the reasons of each and every one.

But what about God? Is there no superpower that can wave a wand and stop all this hurt and destruction happening?

A father figure that will make everything better in the blink of an eye? And if there was, do you think they would make people – young children – suffer?

I feel I have to say 'no' to the idea of a father figure, but it would be nice if it was.

'God' is 'good' and represents the source of energy that we all spring from and return to. This energy is made up from grains of sand in the form of light. Each grain has its own energy, in the same way that a drop of water is just a drop of water, but many drops form a pond, then a sea, and many ponds join and sometimes, depending on how much it has rained, the water can form a deluge and change the way things are forever.

Individual responsibility combines in either a positive or a negative way, as you perceive on earth, but from the centre point there is only energy – neither negative nor positive. Just energy, just the raindrop, just the grain of sand.

Each has its own consciousness and is responsible for its own thoughts and how it uses those thoughts. If that raindrop or grain of sand wishes to have another experience then it may or may not choose to move somewhere else. Each one is equal, each one can decide how they use their free will, but they must take responsibility for whatever they decide to do. There is no imposed punishment – souls (raindrops and grains of sand) make their own judgements about their thoughts and actions, and learn from them to make different thoughts and actions next time, if the original ones did not exercise out in the way they wanted.

There is no angry father figure who wields a dangerous sword and shouts and screams. If there was, that would remove free will. There is no one to shower you with gifts of varying sorts to say, 'well done, you have obeyed my commands!'

You can make that judgement about yourself. You can return to your source to centre yourself and join with other souls and self-impose any sort of reward or punishment that you wish – if that is your choice – but it will not be imposed upon you by one father or mother figure.

Having said that, returning to source is like returning home, and all the familiarity and love and cosiness that you would hope for is there. You get to meet the energy of souls who are important to you, and you meet and exchange views and experiences, but once back at source everyone is equal.

We started off talking about 'evidence' … we seem to have gone a bit off-topic?

Evidence from your point of view is about reminding souls of their source. That they have come from the same source, regardless of their outward appearance on earth. How is one raindrop or grain of sand better or worse than any other? How can one set of beliefs carry supremacy, if everyone comes from the same place? Should one raindrop fall this way or that? Should one grain of sand be made into a sandcastle or a tunnel? It does not matter in the end. Because the sea will wash the sand away and equal it out, because eventually the raindrop will dry up or run into the sea and will evaporate into a cloud and the process will start again. Whatever that raindrop thought, or whatever the grain of sand hoped for, is of importance neither 'here nor there', 'physical nor spiritual', 'heaven nor earth'.

All you can do is to remind the raindrop and the grain of sand that they are part of something bigger. That they will eventually return to their source and there is no point in forcing anything. In time, things will change. In time, the energies that made up those individual souls will meet up again. In time, they will return to source, and at all times there is free will and free thought. Souls must take responsibility for how they use them and the only people who judge them are themselves.

There is no right way or wrong way. No particular pool or puddle to join, no single beach to wait on. You decide. If you find that storms come along and the sand gets blown about too much, or the rain hits the ground too fiercely, then use your free will to find balance. The process of doing this will remain in your soul's energy as learning. Finding balance means that you understand and know what is out of balance – very necessary if you want to maintain it.

But evidence?? How can people remember that what I am telling them is true?

They must use their free will to make the decision to consider that what you are telling them might be true. If they block it then nothing will get through. If they accept everything that everyone tells them then they are not using free will either! They are just accepting as true something that might not be. It is necessary to use discernment and see what matches the knowledge that is placed deeply inside their soul.

Some people might say 'see what your heart tells you'.

You could say that in a manner of speaking, as the soul isn't just held in the head but all over the body, and the heart centres some of the soul's thought activity, as does the human brain whilst on a physical plane.

It is more a case of looking to their soul energy and comparing what they are reading, or seeing, or experiencing, with what is held there. In your world that comes over as a feeling or a deep sense that something is 'right' or 'wrong', but that sort of polarity is not possible when you are back at source. It is hard for me to explain, as I am at the centre of the stick whilst I am speaking to you and you are off-centre. The words we need – well, we do not use 'words', but the thoughts that we express – are related to being in balance. The concept is rather alien to me.

I can honestly feel how tiring all this is. I feel exhausted again today.

We will leave it here. I think I have answered your question about evidence now?

Yes, it is about reminding people that they come from one source and that they are responsible for their actions. Everything will come back to source in the end, but they have free will about how they spend their time when either on the physical or spiritual plane.

Also, we need polarity (which is not possible in the afterlife, because we are so close to source) in order to appreciate the difference between what we want and what we don't want in our lives (or associated with our energy). There is learning in this process – learning we can take with us and we have free will at all times*. No one judges us, but we can judge ourselves.

Lastly, God is about balance – neither negative nor positive. It is not a father figure imposing punishments or lavishing praise. It is not selective about admission. It is purely our source and the combined essence of who we are.

*Whilst reading this back, it did occur to me that people might argue that exercising free will whilst on a physical plane is not possible for everyone. They might be incarcerated or otherwise restricted in their movements, etc.

There is always an opportunity to exercise free will of thought and how someone reacts to something might be the only free will they CAN exercise.

CHAPTER 13
THE COSMOS

It was 8.15 am before I was able to start typing this morning. There were a couple of things I had to attend to first that couldn't wait.

Hello, Battrick.

Are you still there, please? Are we still able to do this today, or am I too late?

We can reconvene tomorrow morning.

I am OK – I would like to do this now, please. I don't want to miss anything. I am sorry I was doing a couple of other things.

That's OK. In this case I understand.

This morning I want to talk about the cosmos.

The sheer vast size of it is difficult to comprehend, which is why I want to be sure you have a clear head and can concentrate on this.

The sheer expanse is something that the human brain – any human brain – can find difficult to absorb. The complexity of it is beyond, way beyond anything in your experience, either in a physical or spiritual world.

I can understand the physical bit, but are you saying that even in a spiritual world, you are not able to see everything in the cosmos?

At many levels, no. That is the case.

At higher levels and closer to source everything is available to you, but not for every single person after death.

So you have seen it?

Yes, I have been privileged to be able to view it from a vantage point, as

I am designated a teacher.

Where do equal opportunities feature here?

To exercise free will, you need to know everything that is possible. If you give a cat free will, he/she will use it to get more food or to play and chase mice in a field. If you give free will to a person, they may decide to buy a very large television set to see their favourite film. If you give free will to someone who has the desire to learn, they will use it to expand their horizons – that is merely what I have done.

Now, shall we continue?

Yes, please.

I have been ABLE to view the cosmos because it was something of interest to me.

Who controls it?

What makes you think it has to be 'controlled'? The cosmos just is. It consists of many planets and stars (far more than anything you could imagine).

Is there just one heaven for all of these planets?

Firstly, not all of them have evolved to contain human or animal life at the same time. A large number (by your standards) do so at the moment (by your time standards), but they are not accessible to you, as they are too far away.

Remember that time works differently here. There is one source, but a number of collection points.

Collection points? This is getting very weird.

Imagine an octopus with very many more legs than eight, and each one stretches out into the distance. You might have attached to the end of a very long tentacle, but it is still the octopus! The collection part (and I am having to choose words carefully, as they do not exist for us) just refers to the fact that souls/energy forms gather at these points. There is no separation if you are holding onto a tentacle or an eye! You are still connecting with source. The octopus example exists just to explain the enormity of the situation, rather than making any comparison with any life form that you can imagine, and certainly has no more connection to a sea creature than a land one.

So in answer to your question 'is there more than one heaven?', for you 'no', but then the word 'heaven' needs more clarity. If you are asking me if life forms distant to your universes have a different experience at death and for a while beyond, I would have to answer 'yes', but they will eventually connect to source. Energy of whatever form converts back to its original source and then mutates into other forms and back again. The original energy source is not diminished or enlarged. It remains as it is and always will be 'source'.

And the different names we have for source include 'God' or any other name that might be commonly associated to mean the same thing.

What else can you tell me about the cosmos?

Does it feel like love? Everyone talks about wonderful feelings of love when they have near-death experiences.

Source is central and neutral. Nothing can hurt you, but nothing can excite you, or irritate you, or elate you. It is the original source and everything else comes out of that. When you break from source you experience other things, but those are in equal measure. Pleasure and pain, loss and connection, rejection and love. None of this is possible whilst attached to source. Instead, there is a renewal of energy that is so encompassing and fulfilling.

Like charging up your mobile phone?

That is something you do every day. Connecting to source is something you might do each millennium – in the abstract sense of time. It is something words do not exist to explain, but it is a greater renewal than dying and being reborn. A wonderful feeling that I have been fortunate enough to experience once.

Once you have reconnected to source, how do you break away again?

Using the word 'break' implies that a separation is painful, which it is not. For every millimetre you are separate there are consequential feelings of separation, but this is not what you would experience as pain.

My experience was undertaken to learn and so I maintained separation as I joined. I intentionally connected, with the intention of staying just to experience it. Once you are close to source, your identity and memory of past, present and future is lost. So my connection to source was not complete and I could only stay for a very short time, so that I could tell others about it.

The loss of personal identity is not considered a loss when joining to source, as personal identity is not such a desirable state. I appreciate that is very difficult to comprehend but being part of source is the fundamental desire for each fragment that has broken away. All fragments are trying to get home.

Why did you not stay, then?

Because I have not reached the required level of evolution that I wish.

OK, but I still don't quite understand why we don't just attach ourselves to source at one of the ends of the octopus's tentacles and just stay there, if it is such a desirable state?

Because that is not what source has in mind for us.

So there is intelligence within the source?

Of course! In the same way that you have an intention for your hand or your eye. You are not separate from your hand or eye, they are a part of you, and if you see a biscuit and want to pick it up, you need both!

I am glad to see you are still putting things into words I can understand and relate to!

The hand and the eye are of more use to you if they know what they can pick up and where they should be looking. Your intention (to pick up that biscuit) is limited, to the extent that you know that a biscuit is something nice to eat and there is one on a plate on a table somewhere, so if you scan around with your eye you will eventually see it and then ask your hand to pick it up.

For source, its experience is limited to the sum of its attached parts. So it has given each part free will, in order to expand and realise all the possibilities available. As energy returns to source, source is expanded to include all the memories and experiences of every fragment of soul energy for all time.

Why would source NOT want to do that?

I think I am beginning to understand.

So, to recap: when you die you go through various stages of evolution, but eventually you return to source?

Yes.

Source is where we all started off and it is the essence of every bit of life on this planet and everything we can imagine?

Yes.

Source has intelligence and wants parts of its energy to separate and be identifiable and have unique experiences, so that when those fragments return, they expand the original source.

There is one source, but it is so vast that it is impossible to comprehend and it stretches out to cover the entire cosmos.

Yes.

At the end-points ...

Let me stop you there: there is no end-point.

What about the example of the octopus tentacles?

That was merely to explain that as vast as the source is, there are variations within it (you might say working on different things), but there is no end – ever.

OK, but it is constantly expanding ... is it getting bigger?

It is getting more expansive, but that is not always related to physical size and in this case there is no physical anyway.

I think, Julie, that for the purpose of your writing, this is as far as we can go on this subject. I only have a limited knowledge of what lies beyond expansive source and it is a suitable 'end-point' for the death experience, as subjects experience many lifetimes before they return to it.

With any story, an author can choose to cover a particular period in history or recite a situation that lasted for a particular number of years. Books do not often tell you everything about a life (or a death) from start to finish. Connection to source is our end-point.

And preparation for death is our starting-point?
Exactly. We have looked at the final destination, which is far beyond anything most people could even start to comprehend. We now need to go back and look at things in more detail.

This we will do next week.

Thank you. I feel exhausted again! But thank you, thank you, thank you.

CHAPTER 14
GHOSTS AND SPIRITS

TUESDAY 9 JANUARY 2018

Hello, Battrick

I asked Battrick if he was there and it was as if he was talking from a long way away – almost from on the top of a hill shouting down, or from an upstairs room. He said he was 'there', but it would have to be tomorrow. No further explanation.

I am sitting here a bit longer to see if I have got that right.

Nothing coming into my head – I get the impression anything I come up with today will be out of my head, rather than from anywhere else. It does feel different.

I suppose at the very least it is an example of what it feels like when he is not there! I am going to sign off for today.

WEDNESDAY 10 JANUARY 2018

Battrick – are you there?

Yes, I'm here. Apologies about yesterday, I was detained.

Is that something you can discuss?

Not exactly, but there was something I had to attend to and let us just say that our arrangement has more flexibility.

OK. I am trying to get a feeling for what people in heaven do all day. Is there anything else you can tell me about what you do?

I am a teacher, just like you. My pupils all have different requirements and, like all good teachers, I must respond and devote energy where it is most appropriate to do so. As our arrangement has a measure of flexibility on both sides, I decided yesterday (or rather, was required) to focus my energy in another direction that would ensure it was used to best effect. Our communication has not suffered, the outcomes are the same. I felt that it was necessary to respond yesterday in another direction, as the outcome might have been changed if I had not.

OK, thank you. I am not complaining, of course! I do hope you understand that?

Yes, you like flexibility and that is part of the arrangement we have.

You said you wanted to understand more about how I spend my time.

As I said, I am a teacher, but here this can take many forms. I am not a teacher in the traditional sense that I sit or stand in a classroom. I interact with energetic souls and help them to find meaning in their experiences both while living (not always conducted on earth) and in the afterlife. This involves showing alternative scenarios and playing out alternative lifetimes.

It all sounds a bit like Charles Dicken's 'A Christmas Carol' and the Ghosts of Christmas Past, Present and Yet to Come.

I was not familiar with that as you typed those words, but now I am – I can obtain knowledge in what seems to you seems like an instant, but to me it takes longer. I suppose you may detect some similarity, but in the book there was a punishment element, and my role is kinder. My work (notice I am not using the word 'job', as this is entirely voluntary and brought about by my wishes and intentions) is to show loving guidance by illustrating through thought pictures what the larger outcomes of situations are. For example, the subject may not have realised everything about a situation and their lack of vision may have caused them to operate in a particular way. My role is to show them that there were alternative scenarios which could have been played out and next time they may wish to use their free will in a different direction.

But this all happens once they are dead?

Not necessarily, it could be while they are alive, through dreams and ideas that I am able to impart.

Is that allowed?

Obviously. There is no single power that exerts authority over others. There is no 'Big Brother' to judge. This is self-governing and self-adjudicating.

Can't that be a bit chaotic?

Only for souls who need some guidance. When souls are closer to source, the most desirable courses of action become more apparent.

What about when people first arrive?

Some remember instantly and resume the 'life' they had before they left. Their family come to meet them and their experiences are discussed within their soul group. When I say 'discussed', it is important to emphasise that words are not needed. This is a transmutation of energy back into the group, so when one soul returns to their soul group, the whole group gains experience and their energies meld. This means that there is a deep and loving understanding on all levels. If the life outcomes were not as the subject might have hoped before leaving, the soul group helps to illustrate the larger picture and learning is enhanced once again. Soul energy fragments being born into an earth or other planetary life is what you would call a 'win-win' situation. Everything is fed back to source and everyone benefits.

Every soul passes into the decompression tank that you seem to find unsettling for some reason, but it is an essential part of the process. The first objective is to raise the soul's energy up to where it needs to be, so that it is aware of the beings of light/other soul energies which are part of their soul group initially and then part of everything connected to source eventually. Some souls float through this process very easily and what you would call quickly; others need more adjustment.

'Adjustment'?

Yes: realignment, decompression, greater vision, call it what you will. It does not change the process.

What happens if a soul does not go into the decompression tank, and does this ever happen?

Some souls are very fearful at death. This can be for a number of reasons, such as death being very unexpected, or they are fearful about what awaits them. They have free will/their souls have free will and if they choose not to traverse to the decompression tank, that is their choice.

Does that mean they stay here as ghosts?

Well, that is another very large subject area, but this is an appropriate time for me to shed some energetic light on that.

It depends what you mean by ghosts!

Am I a ghost?

No, you are a spirit person I am talking to. I would not describe you as a ghost.

Exactly, once having passed through the decompression tank and reunited with their soul group, some souls elect to return to where they lived, their family, attend their funeral, etc., attend family events any time they so wish.

Would you describe them as ghosts?

Strangely, no, I would not, but other people might. I suppose for me it just means they are spirits 'in the right place' just having a bit of an outing!

You could say that. Their intentions are to look in on their family and friends, or witness world events first-hand. They are using their full source energy to make decisions based on a knowledge of all that is (as it is sometimes described). These people have passed through the decompression tank and are aware of both worlds, but know exactly that their rightful place (their current 'home') is within the spiritual realm. I would not refer to them as ghosts, either, although it could be said that sometimes their presence is felt and other people may refer to them as ghosts.

What about people/souls who are said to haunt a place?

Normally, these are souls who have decided for whatever reason not to go into the decompression tank, so their energy remains on the physical plane and they are only aware of earthly energies, but not spiritual ones. They are operating as they would have done when they had a body, but now they have the added 'benefit' – or at least, what they might describe as the 'benefit' of travelling around seemingly unnoticed. These are spirits which are aware of and interact with earthly energy. If they have been around for a very long time in your terms, they will have found out how to use their energies quite effectively and they are able to move objects to make sounds, and generally create a worry and a nuisance for people on earth who become aware of them.

If there is sufficient focus on the spirit energy, then they absorb that energy and can 'appear'. All that is needed is for someone to report about them, write something in a book, carry out what you call a 'séance' or (and this is not advised, as it manifests a great deal of energy that can be used by the spirit) use a Ouija board. So in short, the more attention you give it, the more powerful it becomes! That is why these spirits try to get your attention, as every time you pay attention to them, they become stronger.

Should we attempt to 'move them on'? Tell them to go towards the light and get into the decompression tank?

You can suggest it if you can communicate, but they have free will and will only take this course of action if they believe it will be beneficial to them. If they are concerned, worried about what they have done, or are just afraid, they may decide to (and often do) not go towards it.

When people on earth are afraid of these spirits, is there anything they can do?

First and foremost, avoid giving them too much attention, as you just make them more powerful. Children often notice more than adults and they can often be the first people in a household to do this. They become aware of the energy and start to communicate through thought. This is often where the phenomenon of the poltergeist comes from: children focusing on an energy source and making it more powerful.

Secondly, if the energy has already become undesirable then the household need to express their intention that the spirit should leave. Few people choose to stay where they are not wanted and many will leave on this basis.

For older and more determined spirits, it is often necessary to draw on someone from the spirit world to help the soul into the decompression tank. They will know what thoughts to impart which make this seem like a desirable option. The soul still has free will, but if they are able to see an alternative scenario to the one they are currently living then they normally follow. It may be necessary to call upon a high spiritual being to ensure that the process runs smoothly and that is why people (yourself included) call upon angelic realms. Owing to your mythology, Archangel Michael is a popular choice! But in many cases, other spiritual beings will do as well!

I might call on you!

It is not my speciality, but I have had some success in these matters.

What about spirits that are seen in certain places – particularly where they died, and there seems to be a replay of events? People often report seeing someone standing in the road and then promptly running over them in their car, just to find out there was no one there. Sometimes they say the person looks completely normal and other times they say they appear in grayscale. What is responsible for this?

When a spirit has passed to the spirit world, they may focus on certain events in life and that has the effect of taking them back to when the event took place. Time bends in the afterlife and bears little or no connection to what you experience. It is possible to re-enact the point of death many times, but owing to the difference in time, this event is played out at different points in history. The fact that the spirit is shown to you in grayscale means that they are there just in a thought form. If that was not the case, then playing over the event would not be possible. They are most definitely operating from the spirit world.

Phew. Just for the record, how do you feel about ghost hunters and people who go into old buildings looking for ghosts for entertainment purposes?

There are different levels to this. As we said, the more attention that you focus on a ghost, the more energy you impart to it. Some earth-bound souls are tormented and you could argue that you are making a spectacle of them for earthly amusement. People's sensibilities on earth have, for the most part, realised that mocking the afflicted is not a desirable pastime! Mocking souls when living, dead or earth-bound, or in the spirit world, comes under this category. Particularly when people on earth have a vested interest in keeping a spirit earth-bound for commercial reasons.

If the 'ghost hunt' is carried out in a genuine attempt to understand the phenomenon then that comes into the category of learning. Many people still do not accept the existence of ghosts and prefer to provide themselves with a 'scientific' answer that fits their world-view. Being able to do this by criticising the process and results from such an activity gives them comfort. For others, it can provide the 'proof' that is so needed by earthly souls.

Should we fear ghosts?

You should not fear anyone or anything, but you should exercise discernment, as with everything you do. You would not go out at night with a purse full of money in an area where people are desperate to buy drugs. If you pass one group of people, you will probably be ignored and return home safely with your money intact. If you pass another group, you could find that their desire to buy drugs is much stronger than their respect for you.

The telephone rang at this point, but I felt that it was the end of the communication, anyway. By the time the call was over, Battrick had retreated.

CHAPTER 15
REINCARNATION

Battrick, are you there?

Yes, I am here and we are going to talk about reincarnation.

As a part of death?

As a part of the death process, yes.

OK. What can you tell me?

I then started to experience something very strange – almost as though I was travelling very quickly …

I feel as though I am moving. It is rather as if I am on a train or a plane. Probably a plane, because I seem to be moving at high speed. Actually, it is more like being on a jet fighter. What are you showing me? This is different.

I am demonstrating the movement of time.

Is time moving, or are we?

Both. Everything that ever was, still is. The energy that created it has moved on, but its time impression is still there.

OK, time impression?

The residue that the energy left behind. Its impression on the universe. Light moves more slowly than sound…

(Julie later notes that this is directly opposed to current scientific thought!)

…We are covering large distances in the universe and that is endless, so long after a human physical form has deserted a space, the light impression remains. At this dimension it is possible to see the light impression from things that happened many millennia ago in your dimension.

What about the people energies that made these events happen? Is some essence of them still there?

Not in the way you understand, but those people are connected to those events, or at least the fragments of light energy that were present then are still connected to the light energy of their present form. Some people, you included, can read these light impressions. Some people remember just their own and others can read other people's light impressions – sometimes both, as you can sometimes do.

I know I have sometimes had quite a clear picture of someone's past life. Once I could see a man standing in a trench. It was during the First World War and he oversaw a food store. I knew that he would kill anyone who tried to steal the food, as they were all starving themselves. He was an honourable man and regretted not asking a woman out whom he knew back home. There was regret, resolve and a good deal of his personality that I could understand in the couple of minutes I received this impression.

Well, you were tuning into his light energy. Fragments (and in his case many fragments) of the same energy were carried forward into his current life. That was why you could read it and get such a clear picture. There were what he would have described as 'mistakes' which were included in that life. He wanted to make sure he learned from it and took different actions this time. There are no mistakes. Decisions in one life are taken so that scenarios can play out that help to develop a soul and feed back into the universal energy source.

There is an awful lot to take in here. So, what about when someone spontaneously remembers past lives? What is the purpose/objective of that?

Souls evolve at different rates and have different intentions. It was your intention to come to this life with an ability to be able to access previous lifetimes.

Why did I decide to do that?

So that you could tell people about it and write this book!

Well, I have certainly been very fortunate about remembering and have been given several examples. Not just my own, but through my daughter as well.

Exactly! You knew that you would record this and it would receive a wider reading at some point, either before death or posthumously.

Oh dear, now I need to consider my own demise!

Demise is not the best word to use, as it implies a sinking into the earth, never to be seen again, but as you are realising, death is not like that! The energy of the book we are creating together will go on long after you do. Whether it remains in publication or not is not the issue. When you create something, fragments of its energy remain. The more people read the words and focus on the book, the more energy is associated with it as it impresses on their energy.

Once again, there is a lot to take in.

The more someone engages with something, the more attention (and therefore energy – light energy) is bestowed upon it. The more people who interact with it, the stronger and brighter it becomes. The fact that you will not be on earth when some of this happens is of no consequence – not even to you!

OK, well I am not going to ask you how long that will be, as I may not like the answer.

We are all just passing through this earth plane. When your time is finished, and at a soul level you know exactly when that is, you will return home just like everyone else. Upon your return, you may decide that you would like to return at what will seem to be 'some future point'. If that is what your free will elects to do, then your soul can do that.

So, if I don't get things right this time, I can have another go?

I will ignore the 'if I don't get things right' comment, as I have explained

that you cannot get things wrong, but yes.

So, back to the swirling, fighter-pilot-type journey that you have just taken me on. What is all that about?

That is what it feels like to travel back through what you would call time, but is in fact visiting a dimension of the universe that has passed from current time in the current perception of a person on earth.

We really do not have a clue what is going on when we are on earth, do we?

No, not what is going on outside your limited existence, no. You knew before you were born. You will know when you die, but while you are 'on holiday' on earth, no, you do not realise anything like the full extent of the situation. Your brains are not designed to understand, as it could affect the choices you make and would/could detract from the learning you have decided to undertake and the experiences you have decided you wanted to take back (in energy form) to your soul specialist group.

There are so many questions relating to those few words, but I will start with, 'how does anyone decide what life they can be reborn into?'

Because they have been able to review it in advance. Just as the light energy exists from past lives, it exists in future lives as well.

Well, how can it? It hasn't happened yet!

It hasn't happened yet, only based on your current perception. It has happened before in many different ways! Numerous scenarios are played out before you are born. Some will achieve your aims better than others. You normally forget all this a few hours/days after birth – sometimes in the womb – but everything that your life ever could be exists. That is not to say that you don't have free will to make choices, but those choices are still in existence in their infinite form. What you finally end up doing on earth is only the result of the choices that you make. You cannot do anything wrong; you can only choose something else.

Does it matter what you choose?

Not in the sense that some choices are better than others from a soul point of view. Not in the sense that there is some punishment waiting for you if you pick one thing over another. But in the sense of your intentions and aims before you were born, and the experience in light form that you wish to take back to your soul group, some choices will bring you closer to those aims than others. However, you are not the only person in the universe with the same aim, so if the light memory and experience that you bring back are not quite what you originally intended then there is no issue or problem with that, as another soul will, and it may not have been a strong part of their original intention.

Do we have a choice who we are born to, and who our brothers/sisters and partners will be?

When you go on holiday, how do you decide who to take with you?

Someone who will be fun, who is good in a crisis (maybe) and who would like to go with me.

Well, the decisions you make about who you reincarnate with are not so very different. People often decide to reincarnate in groups. Earth can seem a hostile place when you are in this dimension and surrounding yourself with people you love and who love you is a good idea. That is not to say, of course, that you will always be surrounded by Love Light – of course not, as you would not then give your soul any challenges, but you want to know that people who do love you can be around for support and can be relied upon (to the extent that their soul has this role).

So firstly, can we choose our parents?

Yes, but let us be clear, we may have specific reasons for choosing the people we do and it may not be those people whom we are relying upon. Not all parents can be relied upon to provide the best environment for their children. They are on a path that you might describe as destructive, but they have reincarnated for a particular purpose.

I need to get back to this aspect of the conversation, but I want to talk more about how we select parents. How does all this work?

Remember, everything that ever was or ever could be 'is'. Whatever life path the free will of a soul decides to take, everything already 'is'. As a soul considering reincarnation, it is possible to read all those optional choices in a millisecond of your time. So, depending on the aims and learning and experiences that a soul, or soul group to be more precise, wish to experience, a life is selected that will provide the sort of experiences and learning required.

How does all this work? Is it a bit like a dating site?

More like a database, but a multidimensional one. When a soul wishes to reincarnate, they travel to a place where they can view the database. They do not do this on their own, they are accompanied by members of their soul group and this can take place many hundreds of years in your time before they are born. Soul groups focus on family groups as it makes this work easier. There is a familiarity (literally) about it, but an uncle in one life could be your next-door neighbour or your son's girlfriend in another. The relationships do not have to be linked by earth blood. Why should they be? Therefore, it does not really matter what sex you are or whether the family you are living with are your blood family, or your adoptive family, or the friends you call 'family'.

That is very encouraging.

We are all from one source – regardless of earthly appearance, we are all the same. There are variations and specialisations, as there is no point and no learning if everyone is having the same experience on earth or any other planet over and over again.

I think I know the answer to this, but are you saying that reincarnation on other planets in possible?

Yes, but planets go through different stages, making life more desirable on certain planets at certain times. Soul groups work with one or two planets at what you would understand as the same time. That is not to say that everything a planet ever was or ever will be is not accessible to them, they just normally focus on one area at a time. Currently, this is earth and this is the time span you are experiencing now.

OK, is it possible to go back and rewrite history?
Not for an individual soul as part of this process, but periods in ancient history can be re-experienced anew.

You are going to have to explain that one!
You might understand it as recycling, but to us it is just a way to gain experiences, love light and transmute energy.

An example?
What you are understanding as history has only passed from your view-point. Everything that ever was or could be is still there in energy light form. It has been created so that if souls are reborn into that situation (whether they were in it the first time or not), they can replay events and make different choices to the souls that were there before.

If we take an event such as an earthquake – that only happens on one of your earth days. Souls reborn have lifetimes before and often after the earthquake. The decisions that they took during their earth lives and the free will they experienced will impact on how the earthquake is experienced by them personally. If they survive it then they have a chance to undertake a completely different experience, as their response to it could be different to the one they took before (if they were in fact there before). The people reincarnated with them will be from different soul groups and will have different aims to before. The event that you might call 'historical' is in fact making new history.

I think your question might have been based on your perception of time travel.

I think possibly you are right. When we see science fiction films, occasionally someone travels back in time and they have to be careful not to interact with events that can change the world!

Travelling back in time is not possible in your dimension whilst in a physical body, but it is possible to experience any aspect of anything that ever was or is whilst in the non-physical realm.

To clarify, if a soul while resident in an earth body wishes to experience a period of your history, provided they were connected to it at the time, their soul can leave their physical body and experience it through the spiritual realm. People normally choose to do this through dreams and often it is involuntary from an earthly perception, but it is possible. Few people – although there are a few – have trained themselves to do this, but it is not necessary.

Once back in the spiritual realm, it is possible to travel in soul light form to concentrated light energy points and view everything that ever was, or is, or will be.

So there is not time, but there is place?

Firstly, there is time, just not in the way you experience it. Secondly, there is 'place', which could be described as energy light concentration points.

CHAPTER 16
THINGS I WANTED TO ASK

These questions were asked over several days, starting Wednesday 17 January 2018.

1 Does karma exist?

The idea that if you are good in life then good things come to you?

This is true in terms of energy blobs attracting sympathetic energy dust – like attracts like. However, if you murdered someone in one life it does not automatically mean that you will have a miserable life and be horribly murdered yourself in this one. Or even if you were the kindest person, you are not immune from being unlawfully killed and will not necessarily live the life of a fairy-tale prince or princess!

However, the agenda within which people reincarnate is complex. A soul may agree to reincarnate for a very short amount of time, out of love. A child, for example, who is born with a heart defect, may be around for less than a year, but their birth can bring both joy and sadness to the people around them. There may have been an agreement before the parents were born that this event would take place (although with free will this will always remain only a possibility – the parents may decide not to have any children, for example).

This is a very difficult subject for many people and we have had experience of that scenario in my own family group. Why on earth would a parent want to bring a child into the world, knowing they are only here for a short time? The utter despair and sadness that this brings is so overwhelming and long-lasting that it shadows the rest of their lives.

When they make the decision on earth they do not know, which it is exactly how it must be. Otherwise why would they make it?

There is no switching-off of the lights when someone passes. Their physical body is cast off, but their energy remains. Once they pass, there is no physical pain. Being born into a family can help the development of everyone who met the child. That briefly-reborn soul may not have wanted to spend any longer on earth. They may have felt that their energy life was better served from the other side.

Reasons are complex when people and souls have free will!

2 *What happens to murderers when they pass?*

Unfortunately, we have borne witness to some hideous crimes of the utmost cruelty and we think of the perpetrators as 'evil'. What happens to them?

I want to ask if they go to hell.

As I have said before, if they expect to be punished when they pass over then that is largely what they will experience. They have in fact designed their own version of hell as a sort of punishment, which they feel will help to 'balance the heavenly books' and, for a while at least, that is what they will experience. However, in order to feel the necessity of creating a version of hell for yourself, you probably need to feel some modicum of remorse. If that is the case then the punishment, or should I say self-punishment, will come to an end at some point when the soul feels as though the bad choices they made in their earthly life are spent. The period of perceived time during which the hell continues is dependent on the soul who designed this punishment for themselves.

Not everyone feels remorse. Some people of course feel fully justified in carrying out mass murder – what about them?

Again, whatever they think they will experience can form part of their experience at the moment of death. However, once they have passed, their perspective is broadened and they start to understand the motives of others. Any perceived differences between cultures or beliefs are washed away when that full understanding is achieved.

Can you explain more, please?

Many murders are taking place all over the earth in the name of certain religions. The perpetrators believe wholeheartedly that they are carrying out God's work and that a reward is waiting for them in heaven.

At death, it is quite likely that the soul will experience a vision that is completely in line with what he/she has been told. For a short while at least, this will reinforce the decision to carry out the act and probably end their own life at the same time. This justification may be very important to him or her.

What happens next? This is a very sensitive subject for many people. In view of these awful atrocities, many people would want a suicide bomber to 'burn in hell'.

What other people want is of no consequence. Equal opportunities mean that everyone, whoever they are and whatever they have done, has free will. There are people to guide, but each soul decides their own path. They will soon realise that their actions have not given them any sort of special privilege and that the visions they experienced at death were transitory.

Then what happens?

Whatever they want. Much depends on what their intentions were before birth.

Is there no incentive to be 'good'?

The sort of life that you lead on earth does not buy you special treatment when you pass!

So there really is no karma?

Not in the sense that you understand it, but there is expanded vision. If you fully understand what is really going on and you can see how you used your free will in a way that caused much distress to others, then a soul can start to expand. There will be family soul group members who support and guide, and can show the newly-departed soul the consequence of some of his or her actions. In the heaven environment love and kindness prevail, so energy can be transmuted to be in alignment.

3 Do our pets have an afterlife?

We are from one source and that applies to everything you feel, see, touch, hear and find in your home or garden. Everything eventually returns to source. Our pets often have a very strong connection to us and can be very loyal. Death does not change that. Our pets can be waiting for us, or we can be waiting for them.

Do animals experience the afterlife in the same way?

If you are asking if every living creature on earth has the same afterlife experience, then the answer is no. If an ant dies, it does not have a family waiting to help it evaluate its past experiences. Animals that have shared a human existence in a meaningful way do. So you could find a special horse waiting for you, or your cats and dogs. Simpler life forms have a much quicker transition and are quickly reborn. So the ant that you see today under the sole of your foot will be reborn next season.

Oh dear, that sounds very harsh and might encourage people to step on ants. Don't Buddhists say that you should not kill a living creature, as it might have been your mother in a previous life?

That is not strictly true. The souls of living creatures such as insects (although this does not apply to birds) die and are reborn very quickly into the same or a similar species.

4 When you have a very loving couple who live many happy years on earth and one of them dies a long while before the other, what happens if the one remaining meets someone else? What happens when they get to the afterlife?

There is no judgement, there is no sense of loss; there is recognition and love. There is room for everyone. There is no one saying that you should or should not have married / met someone else / performed a physical act with someone, as it is 'disloyal'.

When you die, you may wish to look back at your earthly life and record the decisions and outcomes in your soul's data bank, and those actions may influence you in another life, but there is no animosity.

5 What about when the other person dies and you have a wife/new partner and husband, or husband/second partner, or husband and wife, all in the same place?

Absolutely nothing out of the ordinary.

6 How does the person who has had more than one partner decide who to spend his or her (after-)life with?

Souls move individually or in groups, their energies can be fragmented and they all have free will. Elements of their energy field in soul form can be in more than one place at once. They also left some of their soul energy in the afterlife when they were reborn on earth. In other words, there is plenty to satisfy everyone.

7 When a close partner dies, can they come back and watch you sleep, or maybe let you feel the sensation of their hand on your face?

Yes. It depends on the motivations on both sides, but this is very possible. The extent to which a spirit can make their presence known is dependent on how strong the link is. That depends on the emotional link during life. If a couple were very close, then yes, of course, they often come back to see how you are doing. In many cases they do not expect you to be aware of their presence, but they may try to get your attention if they think it will be a comfort to you.

8 How can they get our attention?

You might be aware of the sensation of a hand on your face, or you can smell their familiar scent. You might just feel as though someone is standing behind you or to the side of you. You might hear your name as you fall in or out of sleep as they call you. There are numerous ways. They may have to wait until you go to see a medium, or they may decide just to observe from a distance, as appearing to you would be far too upsetting – this is often the case.

9 *How do people know that everything written in this book is accurate?*
The proof is there in their soul. They will feel it. If they do not feel it is right, then it isn't.

But that is a bit vague. Sometimes we don't know what we feel.
Try not to question every word. This book will work on more than one level. There is the conscious level, as you read the words and they pass through your logical mind, and then there is the subconscious level, where the words go into your internal data bank so that they can be recalled later, and then there is the soul level. This is the level that concerns us. Your soul is reminded of something they already know – that is a comfort and a reassurance, and your learning on earth is confirmed. The soul level is the one that counts and that is something you can learn to feel.

10 *Does it ever get boring in the afterlife?*
That is not an emotion we choose to experience.

11 Throughout this book, you say that people can create what they have around them. How easy is this and does it include everything we would know and understand from our perspective, such as cars, wallpaper and cakes, to name a few random items?

It is using your energy to create an illusion. It feels very real, as it does on earth. Everything is just as solid in appearance as it is on earth, if you want to perceive it that way. You can create what you want, but you soon realise that material items are unimportant and not a necessary part of the afterlife. It can take souls a while to learn this, but once they do, they become free.

12 What would you say to people who think the afterlife sounds so wonderful that they should end their lives now and join it?

People who decide to leave their earthly lives prematurely are not seeing all the options available to them. Although there is no punishment here from an external source, when they arrive they are helped to see what they have left behind and how they could have stayed and enjoyed a useful life.

It is not the soul's intention to return to source by hastening the end of the physical life. That means mission aborted, rather than mission accomplished. When a successful mission was going through a rough patch of water, then to abandon everything because you 'thought' worse was on the way is not a good idea. There is learning in the difficult things we face, so abandoning everything you have set up and worked towards to accomplish is not a good idea. It means that you will decide to put yourself through those lessons again.

For the people who believe their lives contain no hope, are full of despair and take the decision to end their lives – there is regret. They are focusing on their difficulties and cannot see their place in the world, or the help that is available – they believe they cannot, but even in those darkest moments there is guidance available that will bring them out of their despair and deliver them into a better life.

Someone is always with you and sending you love. You are never alone and no one ever gives up on you, however bad things appear to be.

13 Do angels and archangels exist? And if they do exist, do they really have wings, and if they do have wings, why do they need them?
There are celestial bodies that carry a higher vibration than others. These bodies are pure light and emit what you would see as a large glow around them – almost blinding, if you could see it.

People on earth have seen this almost blinding glow and have interpreted this as massive wings. They are aware that the human-like image that is portrayed (and this is a convenience, as they can appear in whatever form they like, but something recognisable is less intimidating) has something 'behind' it. That is something very large and bright. As people look upwards for answers, if something 'appears' then it must have come down, and therefore the only point of reference would be a large bird – hence the wings.

Once this image was accepted and there were paintings, etc., the phenomenon (although I am sure you can appreciate it is so much more than that one word implies) of an angelic presence – angels, in other words – was written into human existence.

You see what you expect to see, once you have passed, and if you expect these higher vibrational beings to have wings then that is how they will appear to you. But no, in the traditional sense of what a wing is used for then technically, 'no', they are not required.

14 Can you tell me what they do, please? How do they differ from normal spirits? What is their job?
They have been developed by source as a more powerful entity that can communicate directly with humans and other life-forms throughout the cosmos. As their energy is pure, they are not contaminated by human-like associations or needs.

15 Have they ever lived directly on earth?
Some have and some haven't – some have lived on other planets.

16 Are there any notable angels in human form that I would have heard of?
Yes, and you only need to look at the great prophets in many religions to find some, but it is not our task to list them here. Suffice to say, when in human form they have an agenda and that is leading souls to a higher existence. They are interpreted and misinterpreted, and that can make their task harder. Some have disappeared without any traceable record on earth, whilst others who were not angelic have been exalted to angelic

status as a result of their work, or have been interpreted as such by the populace.

17 Can you describe them, please?

Owing to how they were originally interpreted, and because of the colour of light that can be perceived when they are around, archangels have taken on the names and the attributes which have been associated with them in current culture. They are pure unadulterated energy from source. You can feel their powerful presence and they have abilities beyond anything you can imagine. The names that you are familiar with are Archangels Michael, Raphael, Gabriel.

Then there is another level of angelic presence (which can also be perceived with wings) – these are not directly from source, but are attached to it closely. These have names you would not be so familiar with, but they are very powerful and exist to help people. That is their mission. To save people who, through circumstances, may be set to end their lives before required, or to step in for whatever reason to assist. They have an important role and are more closely aligned to earth than the higher energy angels, but these are the angels you might feel are with you as you go on with your daily life.

18 You don't like me using the word 'heaven', so what would you call it?

Definition of 'Heaven':
First definition (not attributed), which appeared after a Google search on 25 January 2018.

heaven

ˈhɛv(ə)n/

noun

noun: heaven; plural noun: heavens; plural noun: the heavens

A place regarded in various religions as the abode of God (or the gods) and the angels, and of the good after death, often traditionally depicted as being above the sky.

'Those who practised good deeds would receive the reward of a place in heaven.'

There are numerous definitions which people can read, but they all imply that heaven is 'up there' and that entry is restricted on some basis or other. This is categorically not true. Heaven is not 'up there', it is everywhere, including 'here', and it is all-inclusive. There is no hell (other than the hell you make for yourself). To say that it is the abode of God (or the gods) is to imply that superior beings bestow awards (and/or punishment), and this is not true either.

What you are calling heaven is the centre of the source of everything that ever is, was and will be. It is the source of all energy; it is pure and has supreme intelligence. By true definition, it is your source, my source and the source of every microbe you can imagine.

This is not people's current understanding of the term 'heaven', which is why I prefer not to use it.

19 Is there one single message we can obtain from this book that will help in our daily lives here?

To live your life in a more spiritual way. That is not to say that you need to follow any organised religion, or wear long flowing robes and adopt strange customs. It means that you listen to your soul spirit in all things. Your best guide is what some people might call their 'gut feeling', but it is so much more than that. It is your internal guidance mechanism and people on earth often forget to listen to it. Finding that guidance within you takes some practice, but it is there within everyone and they need to learn to switch off from their busy lives and learn to listen.

One very last question.

20 What do you hope to achieve with this book?

That is a good question. I hope that people will read the words with an open heart and 'feel' whether they are right for them at this time. If not, they should put the book down immediately and pass it to someone else, or leave it and pick it up again later. These words work on many levels. For some, they will confirm what they already know. For others, they will be an unbelievable revelation and sometimes, for some people, the words may contain something they decide they would rather not know. There will be people for whom these words represent incoherent ramblings, which are at best delusional and at worst, dishonest and cruel.

People will decide, as they have free will. If you create something you cease to own it; it belongs to everyone. Money may change hands with the physical representation of the article you have created, but once the energy has been moulded in this way then it belongs to everyone. You cannot control who reads it, or their thoughts while they do so.

If you are asking me what I hope to achieve with this book then it is to make it available to as many people as possible, so that they can decide and they have the ability to choose.

CONCLUSION

There was one very significant day in January 2007 when my belief in an afterlife became a 'knowing' that our personality does not die and the true essence of who we are remains forever. From that point, I have not looked back. I can honestly say that 'I do not **believe** in life after death; I **know** there is life after death'.

Despite all the things that had happened to me prior to that point, it was a one-to-one reading with the wonderful medium Gordon Smith that changed everything. At that time, Gordon Smith rarely gave one-to-one readings, but he was offering this exceptional opportunity in the form of a competition on his website. 'Amazingly', my name was selected and I went to London to have a reading that would confirm everything I believed and hoped was true. Gordon brought through my father and it was just as though he was speaking to him at the end of the telephone. The evidence and proof of his continued existence shocked me to the core. I could not verify absolutely everything that Gordon told me immediately, but over the next few days/months I could place almost every tiny detail. The fact that I was being told things that even I didn't know at the time helped to prove to me that this was not a psychic reading (i.e. being picked up from things in my aura) and was most definitely a mediumistic one (being communicated from the afterlife). Gordon also confirmed that I had been speaking directly to my grandmother, who had died several years previously; apparently she was having difficulty maintaining the communication with me and needed to stop because it was draining her energy. This of course helped me to confirm something I had not told a living soul and gave me the confidence to develop my own mediumship, to ensure that the messages I brought through were as accurate as possible.

Moving from 'belief' to 'knowing' rarely happens overnight!

Regardless of where the information in this book originates from, my hope is that the reader will focus on the overall message. The essence of who we are does not die with our physical body. We are never alone, although our departed loved ones do respect our privacy! Love transcends dimensions and we are still connected to the people we love, regardless of which side of life they may reside. Our thoughts matter and it is important to be kind and caring to one another. Most of all, we need to aim to live our lives on earth in a more spiritual way; your heart and soul are your guide.